Subsidiarity
within the
European Community

Federal Trust Report

THE FEDERAL TRUST

The Federal Trust for Education and Research was founded in 1945 to be the research arm of Federal Union. The aim of the Trust is to study the theory and practice of federal government. The principal focus of its work has been the European Community and the United Kingdom's place within it.

The Trust conducts inquiries, promotes seminars and conferences and publishes on a wide range of contemporary issues. Its future work programme includes continuing study of Economic and Monetary Union, a major enquiry into the role of national parliaments within the EC and an exercise in building alternative scenarios for Europe's future. A book on the implications of the Treaty of Maastricht will be published in Spring 1994. The longer term objective of the Trust is to contribute towards a constitutional settlement for the New Europe.

The Trust also sustains a major programme of European civic education for sixth forms, universities and young leaders.

The Federal Trust, which is chaired by John Pinder, is the UK member of TEPSA (the Trans-European Policy Association).

Subsidiarity within the European Community

A Federal Trust Report

Edited by Andrew Duff

Published by the Federal Trust for Education and Research
158 Buckingham Palace Road
London SW1W 9TR
Telephone 071-259 9990
Fax 071-259 9505

ISBN No. 0-90157342 6

The Federal Trust is a registered charity

Produced by PSI Publishing, London NW1 3SR

Printed in Great Britain by BPCC Wheaton's, Exeter

CONTENTS

About the Authors

Andrew Duff was appointed Director of the Federal Trust in January 1993, having been a Senior Research Fellow. He has worked for the Hansard Society, at Cambridge and Brussels Universities and as a consultant on many aspects of European Community affairs. He has been a Westminster and European parliamentary candidate for the Liberal Democrats, and a Cambridge City Councillor 1982-90. He is a member of the Board of the UK European Movement.

Michael Burgess has recently left Keele University and is now Senior Lecturer in Politics at Hull University. He is a member of the Comparative Federalism and Federation Research Committee of the International Political Science Association. He has published widely on the history and evolution of federalist thought, and is currently writing a book on the roots of the British federal tradition.

Anthony Cary was deputy head of the Cabinet staff of Sir Leon Brittan, Vice-President of the EC Commission 1989-93. He was previously First Secretary and Head of Chancery British High Commission, Kuala Lumpur, Singapore (1986-1988) and Private Secretary to Malcolm Rifkind and Linda Chalker, Ministers of State in the Foreign & Commonwealth Office with responsibility for Europe and Africa respectively (1984-1986).

Alan Trench studied politics at Bristol University, where he joined the Young European Movement, and at Boston, Massachusetts. He is now an articled clerk with Messrs Browne Jacobson, solicitors, in Nottingham.

Paul Bongers is one of Europe's leading practitioners of cooperation between local government within the EC and the Council of Europe. He is currently the Director of the Local Government International Bureau.

Annemie Neyts-Uyttebroeck is Member of the Belgian Parliament and was President of the Flemish Liberal Party (PVV). She was President, PVV City of Brussels 1977-85, co-President, Second Congress of Flemish Brussels Citizens, 1979-81. She was elected Deputy in 1981 and was Secretary of State for the Brussels Region 1981-85. She was Vice-President then President of PVV women until 1982 and was a Local Councillor for Brussels in 1983.

Carles Gasòliba i Böhm has been a Member of the European Parliament for Catalonia since 1986, where he sits in the Liberal, Democratic and Reformist Group. He is a member of the Executive Committee of the CDC (Democratic Convergence Party of Catalonia). He was formerly Senior Economist at the Banco Catalana, 1968-1980, and was a lecturer at the Autonomous University of Barcelona, 1970-1980.

1

Dr Otto Schmuck was recently appointed as Head, European Affairs Department, in the Rhineland-Palatinate Ministry for Federal and European Affairs. He was formerly Deputy Director of the Institute for European Politics, Bonn. He is Visiting Professor at the College of Europe in Bruges; and Visiting Lecturer, University of Mainz.

Councillor Sir John Chatfield is President of the Consultative Council of Regional and Local Authorities with the EC Commission. He was chairman of the Policy Board of the Local Government International Bureau; Vice-President of the British Section of the International Union of Local Authorities (IULA) and the Council of European Municipalities & Regions (CEMR); UK representative on IULA Executive Committee and Vice-President of CEMR since 1989. He was leader of UK Delegation to the Standing Conference of Local and Regional Authorities of Europe in 1989 and Founder Chairman of the International Council of Local Environmental Initiatives in 1990.

Andrew Scott is Jean Monnet Senior Lecturer in the Economics of the European Community at the Europa Institute of the University of Edinburgh. **David Millar**, is a former Clerk of the House of Commons and Senior Officer of the European Parliament, is now an Honorary Fellow at the Europa Institute, Edinburgh. They have both been involved in the work of the Scottish Constitutional Convention.

Alex Salmond has been the SNP Member of Parliament for Banff and Buchan since 1987, and became the Senior Vice Convener and Deputy Leader of the Scottish National Party in late 1987. He is now national convener and is the Party's Parliamentary Spokesman on Treasury affairs, constitutional matters, energy and fishing. He is also a member of the Westminster select committee on energy.

Henry McLeish was elected Labour Member of Parliament for Fife Central in 1987. He is Shadow Spokesman on Scottish Affairs. He was formerly Chairman of the Education Committee, Fife Regional Council (1978-82) and Leader of the Council 1982-87.

James Wallace was elected as Liberal Member of Parliament for Orkney and Shetland in 1983. In June 1992 he was elected as Leader of the Scottish Liberal Democrats and speaks for the Party on Scottish affairs in the House of Commons. He is also a member of the Scottish Constitutional Convention.

Malcolm Grant, who comes from New Zealand, is Professor of Land Economy in the University of Cambridge. He was appointed a member of the Banham Commission on Local Government Reform in 1991.

2

Councillor Elgar Jenkins was appointed in 1991 as Conservative Leader of the Association of District Councils, and Vice-Chairman, Local Government Advisory Committee. He is Chairman of the Bath District Health Authority, having been a Deputy Headmaster in Secondary Education until taking early retirement in 1988. He was formerly Vice Chairman of the Bath Conservative Association and Chairman, Western Area Education Advisory Committee. He was also former Mayor, Leader, Chairman of Education, Housing & Personnel of Bath City Council.

Councillor Jeremy Beecham is the Chairman of the Association of Municipal Authorities, and Director of the Northern Development Company. He was formerly member of the Labour Party Local and Regional Government Sub-Committee 1971-1983, and served on the NEC/Shadow Cabinet Working Party on Future of Local Government 1984-1987. He was Vice-Chairman, Northern Regional Councils Association 1986-91; Deputy Chairman, and then Vice-Chairman of the Association of Municipal Authorities from 1984 to 1991, when he become Chairman. He is currently a Senior Partner in the law firm Alan, Henderson, Beecham & Peacock.

Andrew Stunell is Political Secretary of the Association of Liberal Democrat Councillors, and Chair of the Liberal Democrat Working Party on Local Government Reform. He is a former City and County Councillor and was Vice-Chair of the Association of County Councils from 1985-91. He has written publications on local government reform, council procedures, and on making a 'balanced' Council work.

3

Acknowledgements

The Federal Trust is most grateful to the Joseph Rowntree Charitable Trust without whose support this project would not have taken place. My predecessor Gary Miller set up the enquiry and Nicholas Blow helped me bring it to fruition. The College of Europe, the Institut für Europäische Politik and the Institut de la Décentralisation invited me to give papers to conferences on the subject. Daniel Wincott of Warwick University gave me the benefit of his advice.

The Federal Trust is especially indebted to all the contributors tthis report and to those who participated in our conference *Subsidiarity in Britain* in London on 9 December 1992.

In the course of the project I transmuted from being rapporteur of this project to Director of the Federal Trust. My opinions, however, remain my responsibility.

Andrew Duff
London
August 1993

EXTRACTS FROM THE TREATY ON EUROPEAN UNION

Article A (new)

By this Treaty, the High Contracting Parties establish among themselves a European Union, hereinafter called 'the Union'.

This Treaty marks a new stage in the process of creating an ever closer union among the peoples of Europe, in which decisions are taken as closely as possible to the citizen.

The Union shall be founded on the European Communities, supplemented by the policies and forms of cooperation established by this Treaty. Its task shall be to organize, in a manner demonstrating consistency and solidarity, relations between the Member States and between their peoples.

Article B (new)

... The objectives of the Union shall be achieved as provided in this Treaty and in accordance with the conditions and the timetable set out therein while respecting the principle of subsidiarity as defined in Article 3b of the Treaty establishing the European Community.

Article 3b (new)

The Community shall act within the limits of the powers conferred upon it by this Treaty and of the objectives assigned to it therein.

In areas which do not fall within its exclusive competence, the Community shall take action, in accordance with the principle of subsidiarity, only if and in so far as the objectives of the proposed action cannot be sufficiently achieved by the Member States and can therefore, by reason of the scale or effects of the proposed action, be better achieved by the Community.

Any action by the Community shall not go beyond what is necessary to achieve the objectives of this Treaty.

Article F (new)

... The Union shall provide itself with the means necessary to attain its objectives and carry through its policies.

Article 235 (unamended)

If action by the Community should prove necessary to attain, in the course of the operation of the common market, one of the objectives of the Community and this Treaty has not provided the necessary powers, the Council shall, acting unanimously on a proposal from the Commission and after consulting the European Parliament, take the appropriate measures.

— Part One —

CHAPTER ONE

Towards A Definition of Subsidiarity

by Andrew Duff

Britain in Europe

To define 'subsidiarity' is a difficult but reasonable task. In the long-standing and continuing debate about Britain's place in Europe, any agreement on what words meant would be progress indeed. The British European debate has taken on surrealist qualities, filled with dissembling and peppered with jargon and euphemism. First, those politicians who are blatant, self-confident and irretrievable nationalists — once plain 'anti-Marketeers' — are now dubbed 'Euro-sceptics'. Second, the government, which appears to be at best truly sceptical about European integration and at worst rather cynical, claims to be "at the heart" of Europe. Third, British European federalists, an apparently rare public phenomenon, are caricatured as unpatriotic extremists and bogeymen.

A definition of subsidiarity agreed by the three sides to the debate, therefore, would be a prize worth having — were it only to enhance the integrity of the language. In addition, nationalists would find subsidiarity a useful tool to constrain the power of Brussels, just as Pope Pius XI in *Quadragesimo Anno* (1931) called it in aid to restrain Mussolini.[1] Europeanists, for their part, need subsidiarity to make the Community work better. And all European citizen-electors need subsidiarity simply to help them know more about how they are governed, by whom and from where.

This is a report of a Federal Trust study of the question of subsidiarity conducted in 1992/93. Many of the practical results of our enquiry will be fed into our continuing work in the run up to the next constitutional reform of the European Community (EC) in 1996. Our preliminary conclusion, however, is that the introduction of the concept of subsidiarity will be of lasting value to practitioners and observers of European integration, and that, depending partly on what else survives, it may prove to be the most important innovation of the Treaty of Maastricht.

The Maastricht Process

The Treaty of Maastricht constitutes one of the most difficult chapters in the history of the European unification. The Single European Act, which greatly extended the powers of the Community, had been signed in February 1986 and came into force on 1 July 1987. Apart from a rather idiosyncratic constitutional

In June 1988 the European Council at Hanover gave instructions for work to begin on preparing new plans for Economic and Monetary Union (EMU). By the following June, on the basis of a report by a committee chaired by Jacques Delors and despite Margaret Thatcher's obvious reservations, the heads of government meeting in Madrid felt ready to call for the convening of a new Intergovernmental Conference (IGC) for the further revision of the Treaties. The realization of EMU, which was to begin in 1990, would have to "take account of the parallelism between economic and monetary aspects, respect the principle of subsidiarity and allow for the diversity of specific situations".[2] Further Treaty revision for EMU was envisaged under Article 102a of the Single Act. This was confirmed by the Strasbourg Council in December 1989, and by the following October, in Rome, the European Council reached agreement among 11 Member States on the adoption of a single currency, and the beginning of Stage Two of EMU in 1994.

Article 30 (12) of the Single Act prescribed a review of the Treaty in the field of foreign policy cooperation after five years — in other words, 1992. But the Community's flight towards EMU coincided with the collapse of the Soviet Union and the unification of Germany. Negotiations began with the EFTA countries for the creation of the European Economic Area. In April 1990 Chancellor Kohl and President Mitterrand decided to force the pace of political reform. So two IGCs, one on EMU and the other on Political Union, were opened at Rome on 15 December. They were to work in parallel towards the single goal of establishing a veritable European Union. A year later in Maastricht the European Council finished the work of the IGCs. The Treaty on European Union — with its three pillars of EMU, Foreign and Security Policy and Interior Affairs — was signed at Maastricht on 7 February 1992.

Subsidiarity was enshrined explicitly in new clauses. Article A of Title I (Common Provisions) welcomes the new stage in European unification "in which decisions are taken as closely as possible to the citizen". Article B says that the Treaty's objectives shall be achieved "while respecting the principle of subsidiarity as defined in Article 3b". Much of the subsequent controversy about the meaning of subsidiarity turned on the practical meaning of Article 3b of Title II (Provisions amending the Treaty of Rome). Article 3b says:—

> "The Community shall act within the limits of the powers conferred upon it by this Treaty and of the objectives assigned to it therein.

> "In areas which do not fall within its exclusive competence, the Community shall take action, in accordance with the principle of subsidiarity, only if and in so far as the objectives of the proposed action cannot be sufficiently achieved by the Member States and can therefore, by reason of the scale or effects of the proposed action, be better achieved by the Community.

> "Any action by the Community shall not go beyond what is necessary to achieve the objectives of this Treaty."

Douglas Hurd, the UK Foreign Minister, claims it was he who caused at the IGC the last sentence to be detached from the previous paragraph — thereby rendering subsidiarity "in its fully developed form" applicable both to shared or parallel EC competence as well as to exclusive EC competence. He called this "the necessity test".[3]

Subsidiarity in the Maastricht IGCs

In the course of the IGCs, the EC Commission had led the debate about subsidiarity. In its formal *Opinion on Political Union* of 21 October 1990 the Commission proposed that the principle of subsidiarity should be written into the Treaty. It selected carefully the areas in which the EC should be given more power, and these chiefly related to making the Single Market operate fully and effectively, and concerned in the main social affairs, free movement of people and infrastructure networks. The Commission was at pains to emphasise not the redefinition of the powers of the Community, but the improvement of the decision-making procedure — mostly by a greater use of qualified majority voting in the Council. But it accepted that the transfer of however few national competencies to the EC level needed to be justified by rhyme and reason:—

> "The question of subsidiarity is closely linked to the redefinition of certain powers. The Commission considers that this common-sense principle should be written into the Treaty, as suggested by Parliament in its [1984 Spinelli] Draft Treaty on European Union. It should serve as a guideline for the institutions when, under a new Article 235 freed from its purely economic purpose, they have to take a unanimous decision of principle on new Community action in pursuit of general Treaty objectives. Compliance with the principle could be checked by a retrospective control of the institutions' activities to ensure that there is no abuse of powers."[4]

The Commission's plug for subsidiarity was closely related to its desire to simplify EC law. (Unfortunately, this estimable proposal to clarify and rationalize EC law was dubbed a 'hierarchy of norms'. It is possible that the more grisly aspects of the Maastricht process may have been avoided had the Commission from the outset preferred plain language to jurists' jargon. 'Hierarchy of norms' did not last the Maastricht IGC, so we can do better next time round. 'Subsidiarity' itself hardly trips off the tongue, but as it has survived we must try to use and understand it.)

Under the Commission's proposals for a legislative hierarchy, EC law would confine itself to the core of the matter in hand. Were EC legislation to be restricted to the basic elements of substance, national legislation could bear on the technical details of implementation. The variety of types of EC law would diminish and the complexity of EC decision-making procedure reduce. In particular, argued the Commission, the EC Directive — "currently a hybrid instrument of ambiguous status" — could be abolished.[5] A Community act would rest at the pinnacle of this regulatory hierarchy. Its sole purpose would be to establish legal principles and lay down, on a case by case basis, the division of tasks between EC institutions and member governments. The hierarchy, according to the Commission, was necessary for the application of the principle of subsidiarity which meant that "what cannot be done better at Community level at the implementation stage should be left to national authorities". Unlike the existing jumble of EC acts, regulations, directives, decisions, opinions and recommendations, all EC law under the new régime would be binding in its entirety and directly applicable irrespective of whether it was to be implemented by member governments or EC institutions. All EC law could be made jointly by the Council and Parliament. The Commission would retain sole right of legislative initiative, and acquire the sole right of executive power.

Perhaps it was not surprising that the IGC, and particularly Denmark and the UK, rejected the hierarchy of norms proposal. The Commission's repeated assertions that the introduction of the hierarchy would greatly strengthen the efficiency and transparency of the supranational decision-making procedures backfired. Firstly, clarification of the Community's legal acts would have exposed the illogicality of its numerous legislative procedures. Secondly, clarification of the rules for the implementation of EC law would have opened up the whole question of 'Comitology' — the debate between choice of regulatory, advisory and management committee in the operation of EC policy. Few member governments had the stomach for the fundamental reappraisal of the institutional set-up of the Community that was implied by the hierarchy of norms proposal. That the imposition of the hierarchy would have served to unsettle the institutional balance ran counter to the majority view within the IGC. For some years EC governments have tended to prefer the choice of a Directive as a legislative form (binding as to the objective but permissive as to the choice of forms and method) to that of the Regulation (having general application). The Council has continued to insist, under Article 145 of the Treaty, on reserving to itself certain executive powers. Maastricht therefore makes no change to these fundamental matters, and leaves the power to implement EC law shared uneasily — and argued about fiercely in Comitology — between Council and Commission.

Although the Commission did manage to acquire a significant commitment in a Declaration attached to the Treaty that the 1996 IGC will return to the question of creating a legislative hierarchy, Maastricht itself leaves both the executive and the legislative procedure of the Community complex and cumbersome. The application of the principle of subsidiarity is certainly impaired by the Treaty's failure to set out clearly the distribution of power between the supranational and national levels of government. Genuine co-decision between Council and Parliament is introduced, but not comprehensively. Legislative power is still weighted in favour of the Council; executive decisions are still blurred; and Parliamentary control is still weak.

The Commission's proposal to amend Article 235 also failed. This crucial Article of the Treaty of Rome allows the Council to arrogate to itself new powers.[6] It is a way of expanding the powers of the Community without amending the Treaty. It may only be deployed in pursuit of EC objectives, but that, of course, is an ever wider brief — especially in the hands of an assertive European Council. The Commission was not the only institution to be thwarted in the reform of Article 235. The European Parliament under Maastricht remains unable to share in the vital decisions of the Council to expand EC competence.[7] Under Article 235 Parliament shall be consulted only. Likewise under Article 236, which lays down procedures for the revision of the Treaties, the European Parliament's impotence remained amended by Maastricht (Article N).

Long before the heads of government arrived at Maastricht on 10 December 1991 to inscribe subsidiarity in the Treaty, therefore, we have two major paradoxes. There was to be no simplification of EC law and procedures. And member governments in the Council retained the exclusive right to change the constitution more or less as they wanted. Whatever subsidiarity may be, therefore, it is to be applied within a European Community that is ministerial rather than parliamentary in character. Whatever subsidiarity can do, it cannot by itself rectify the EC's structural problems. Although, as we shall argue, subsidiarity is a federalist concept, it sits uneasily in a European federal system that is not comprehensive, not fully democratic and still not working very well.

No wonder, then, that the discussion about the meaning of subsidiarity was confused. How could governments pretend to want a more democratic and decentralized Community when they rejected the main proposals of the Commission and Parliament to make it so? The truth, of course, is that member governments other than Germany realized the importance of subsidiarity only late on in the IGCs, and for different and contradictory motives. And it was only after the Treaty was signed and the ratification process stalled that subsidiarity came into its own.

Subsidiarity and the Ratification of Maastricht
In his formal annual presidential address to the European Parliament, on 12 February 1992, Jacques Delors confined his remarks about subsidiarity to qualify his assertion that the Commission would exploit fully the EC's new powers attained at Maastricht:—

> "It is vital that we make the most of these powers. Not that the Community should regulate everything. On the contrary, its role should be to provide impetus, to innovate, taking a back seat when joint action can develop without its technical or financial intervention."[8]

In Britain, the Second Reading of the Maastricht Bill took place on 20-21 May. John Major, the newly re-elected Prime Minister said that many people were anxious that decision-making in the Community is becoming too centralized.

> "The Maastricht Treaty marks the point at which, for the first time, we have begun to reverse that centralizing trend. We have moved decision-taking back towards the Member States in areas where Community law need not and should not apply. ... The future of Europe is now based on a different foundation. It is based on free trade and

11

competition, on openness to our neighbours, on a proper definition of the limits of the power of the Commission, and on providing a framework for cooperation between Member States outside the Treaty of Rome. That is the Conservative vision of Europe; it is where the future of Europe will lie; and it is a future based on Conservative principles."[9]

On 2 June, however, Denmark voted no to Maastricht, and the European Community was precipitated into one of its biggest crises. The debate about subsidiarity was now engaged almost in panic. The Danish Foreign Minister, Uffe Elleman-Jensen, was foremost in developing the notion that subsidiarity had to be more than just a technical concept. It was, he argued, a sense of openness, clarity and "nearness" that would persuade the Danish people to change their minds about the Treaty. A European Council at Lisbon at the end of June instructed the Commission to work away on the application of subsidiarity to the working of the Community. The French referendum in September, although positive, was only just so. The political crisis in Europe deepened. Large-scale currency speculation and political mismanagement combined to force sterling and the lira out of the Exchange Rate Mechanism (ERM). The commitment of the UK government to ratify the Treaty appeared to falter, and Maastricht was only saved in the House of Commons on 4 November by the few votes of the minority Liberal Democrats.

At once, the term subsidiarity began to flourish in EC statements and documents. The European Parliament called for the establishment of an Interinstitutional Agreement on subsidiarity. The Commission proposed that the Community's financial regulations should be adapted to insist on greater justification and transparency in the EC budget. The UK Presidency called an emergency meeting of the European Council in Birmingham on 19 October expressly to address the problem of public disquiet with Maastricht. The leaders declared their intention to respond to public concerns by demonstrating more clearly the benefits of European integration. This would involve extending the role of national parliaments, making more visible the work of the EC institutions — and in "bringing to life" the principle of subsidiarity. The Commission promised to consult more widely and systematically on draft legislation. The Council should follow the Commission and consider ways of opening up some proceedings to the public gaze. The European Council declared: "We want Community legislation to become simpler and clearer".

Although zealous for subsidiarity, the Birmingham European Council made little more progress than its Lisbon precursor, and left the real decisions to the next, planned for December in Edinburgh. On 27 October the Commission adopted a ten page communication on the matter.[10] Its express purpose was to attempt to link again what Maastricht had effectively de-coupled — the three issues of democracy, subsidiarity and open government. Referring to the implementation of Article 3b, the Commission asserted that subsidiarity should "help to assure the citizen that decisions will be taken as closely as possible to the citizen himself, without damaging the advantages which he gains from common action at the level of the whole Community and without changing the institutional balance".

In areas where competence is not exclusively held by the EC, the test of "comparative efficiency" should be applied. EC action should always be proportional to the dimension of the issue at hand. The Commission returned to the question of type of legislation and administration, and introduced the question of the management of EC policy by subnational, regional authorities. Boldly, the Commission said that the "first application in law of this essentially political principle is to be found in the relationship between some of the Member States and their regions, where it takes various forms depending on their constitutional requirements. In the Community context, subsidiarity means that the functions handed over to the Community are those which the Member States, at the various levels of decision-making, can no longer discharge satisfactorily. Any transfer of powers must have due regard for national identity and the powers of the regions".

Subsidiarity, recalled the Commission, was enshrined both in Article B of the Maastricht Treaty and in Article 3b. "Subsidiarity is a dynamic concept in the Community system. Far from putting Community action in a straitjacket, it allows it be expanded where circumstances so require and, conversely, to be restricted or abandoned where it is no longer justified." Subsidiarity only applies to the exercise of powers not to the conferment of them, which is a constitutional matter. Despite the distinction drawn in Article 3b between the exclusive and shared powers of the Community, it was more difficult to draw in practice. Community action must never be out of proportion. "The text of the Treaty cannot be interpreted so broadly as to leave common sense out of account."

Although the Commission reaffirmed its commitment to the creation of a hierarchy of norms, it recommended that in the meanwhile Directives should return to their original and intended format — in other words, as framework law. Regulations should be used only where uniformity is required. The Commission also expressed its preference for decentralized management procedures. National and regional authorities, however, would need to be responsible for the administration and supervision of EC matters according to strictly uniform criteria if this were to be achieved.

In reaction to British government remarks at the Birmingham summit, the Commission saw fit to sound a warning note about the conditions under which it was prepared to implement subsidiarity. Subsidiarity must not be used to obstruct the decision-making process. It must take its place along side consideration of the merits and the legal basis of a particular measure. It must be subject to the same voting procedures. The Commission recalled its right to withdraw a draft proposal if either the Council or Parliament contravened the principle of subsidiarity. Finally the Commission accepted the need for an Interinstitutional Agreement on subsidiarity procedures in which it would commit itself to use where possible the framework directive as well as to the techniques of mutual recognition of standards (rather than harmonization). The Commission would pay particular attention to the views of national parliaments on subsidiarity. All the institutions should be made to attach a recital to draft legislation justifying their proposals in terms of subsidiarity.

Meanwhile Denmark's political parties had worked out a difficult compromise position which, if accepted by the forthcoming Edinburgh summit, would be put to the Danish people in a second referendum. The Danish document, of 30 October, put great emphasis on the need to arrive at a satisfactory and binding agreement on the limitation of EC competence

Subsidiarity and the European Parliament

The Commission's communication of October 1992 formed the basis of negotiation between national officials and the Council secretariat. It was also debated by two interinstitutional conferences, made up of the three presidents of the Council, Commission and Parliament, Tristan Garel-Jones, Jacques Delors and Egon Klepsch. These meetings had been regular features during the IGC, and their reconvening now demonstrated the importance attached to making sense of subsidiarity.

Under the guidance of Altiero Spinelli, the Parliament had first investigated subsidiarity at the time of its influential 1984 *Draft Treaty establishing the European Union*. The Preamble spoke of the Treaty's intentions to "entrust common institutions, in accordance with the principle of subsidiarity, only with those powers required to complete successfully the tasks they may carry out more satisfactorily than the States acting independently".

In the run up to Maastricht, Parliament appointed the eminent Valéry Giscard d'Estaing as rapporteur on the question of subsidiarity. In April 1990 Giscard proposed a new Article 3a to define the principle, as follows:—

> "In carrying out these activities, the Community shall undertake only such tasks the realization of which requires its intervention because, by virtue of their magnitude or effects, they transcend the frontiers of the Member States or because they can be undertaken more efficiently by the Community than by the Member States acting separately".[11]

Moreover, in its resolution on the matter in November 1990 the Parliament also proposed a new Treaty Article 172a to allow specifically for the institutions or a member government to challenge a measure in the Court of Justice for an alleged breach of the subsidiarity rules. The challenge would have to take place after the measure had passed through all its legislative stages but before coming into force.[12]

As the Parliament's rapporteur, however, Giscard sought to go further and proposed that the new Treaty list the actual division of policies. He clearly

14

believed that a technical definition of the separation of competencies between the Community and its Member States was possible even at the current stage of European integration. His view was that qualitative and quantitative criteria of subsidiarity could be set against which to judge the efficiency of doing something at one level or another.[13] But Giscard's was a more precise definition of subsidiarity than either the Commission or, in due course, the European Council were to allow. And in November 1992 the Parliament adopted a resolution which supported in large measure the more pragmatic approach of the Commission in October. MEPs preferred their subsidiarity to be generally justiciable rather than directly applicable. They stressed the need to protect the *acquis communautaire* and institutional balance. Subsidiarity should in no circumstances jeopardize the Commission's right to initiate legislation nor lead to the introduction of a prior or parallel mechanism of the Council to second-guess the conventional decision-making procedure.

Edinburgh and After
The European Council convened in the Royal Palace of Holyroodhouse in Edinburgh on 11-12 December 1992. Edinburgh was described felicitously in an official handout as "one of the capital cities of the United Kingdom". The choice of Edinburgh, the brief continues, was "a dramatic success, helped by the imaginative efforts of all concerned in Scotland". On the second day of the summit, 25,000 Home Rule demonstrators marched along Prince's Street and up the Mound. The winter sunshine caught the European flags of blue and gold amid the regiment of blue and white saltires of St Andrew.

Meanwhile, back at the Palace, the UK government was striving to achieve one of its overriding objectives. This was to get an agreed definition of subsidiarity that would allow it to claw back to London certain powers conceded in (presumably) weaker moments to Brussels. The government's motives were twofold: first, to reinforce Conservative backbench support for the Maastricht Bill in the House of Commons and, second, to justify its continuing campaign against federalism. Ironically, the Tory nationalists in the Commons tended to accept the federalist interpretation of subsidiarity (and, indeed, of the Treaty as a whole), and remained contemptuous of the protestations of ministers that the Treaty had killed off a federal Europe. Ultimately, therefore, much of the UK government's campaign against federalism was futile. It convinced few.

The British presidency of the EC during the last six months of 1992 was less than a conspicuous success. The continuing quixotic battle against federalism and the mismanagement of the currency crisis jarred against John Major's claim to be 'at the heart of Europe'. By the time of Edinburgh, the UK's reputation in the Community was dangerously low, and Major could afford to take few risks if he was to succeed in avoiding isolation. Britain's partners, and especially the governments of the smaller countries, were determined not to let the UK destabilize the institutional balance of the EC. Above all, the Eleven refused to entertain the possibility of a new institutional mechanism to allow the Council to prejudge legislation on the grounds of subsidiarity alone.

Another point of contention was whether to interpret subsidiarity simply as it is in Article 3b (technical efficiency, objectivity and proportionality) or whether Article A (closeness to the citizen) should be deployed as well. Here the European Council followed the line of the Commission's paper of October and of the European Parliament. The European Council cleverly distinguished between Article 3b as "general principles of Community law" and Article A as "a basic principle of European Union". It went on to assert that "making the principle of subsidiarity and Article 3b work is an obligation for all the Community institutions, without affecting the balance between them". In short, the British government's attempt to hobble the Commission backfired. The European Council leant towards a federalist interpretation of subsidiarity, and, although it dropped references to subnational authorities, its final communiqué on the matter followed in many instances the Commission's October memorandum. The *Edinburgh Annex* is reprinted in full as **Appendix One**. As a manual to the machinery of subsidiarity, it is a significant document.

The European Council confirmed that subsidiarity cannot be used to challenge the primacy of EC law, nor to call into question Article F(3) of Maastricht according to which the "Union shall provide itself with the means necessary to attain its objectives and carry through its policies". It calls subsidiarity a "dynamic concept", allowing the powers of the EC to fluctuate according to circumstances. Even where EC action is excluded, member governments are reminded of the need to respect EC objectives. Subsidiarity does not have direct effect, but is "subject to control by the Court of Justice, as far as matters falling within the Treaty establishing the EC are concerned". Subsidiarity will not apply where the EC has specific obligations, such as competition policy, the need to enforce EC law and to account for EC expenditure.

In areas of shared competence between the EC and national level (that is, almost everything else), discretion will be needed. The EC must not try to avoid the implications of certain articles of the Treaty (for example, Articles 126 to 129 on education, training, culture and health) against harmonization measures by using the catch-all Article 235, but must instead work through and possibly subsidise the cooperation of national authorities.

The *Edinburgh Annex* lays down guidelines for the application of Article 3b. Simply, these involve assuring that:—

(1)   a clear legal basis for the proposed measure shall be established from the outset;
(2)   transnational aspects are involved;
(3)   non-EC action will harm the market or other EC interests;
(4)   EC action will establish clear benefits according to qualitative and quantitative indicators.

The EC's recent prejudice against regulatory harmonization is confirmed, and, where inevitable, these should only be in the form of minimum standards. Financial and administrative burdens should be as light as possible. EC law should be framework in character, leaving much discretion to national implementing arrangements. The amount of EC law should be kept to a minimum and should not apply to all Member States unless all are affected. In addition, the Commission promises to consult more widely, including on the application of Article 3b, by a Green Paper procedure, and will make an annual report on subsidiarity. The UK's request for a separate 'first reading' of any draft measure by the Council with early and simplified blocking powers was turned down flat. Instead, conventional Council voting and rules of procedure will apply to the application of Article 3b, and the Parliament's Opinion will still be required at first reading, along with the Council's reaction. Moreover, "care should be taken not to impede decision-making in the Council and to avoid a system of preliminary or parallel decision-making".

Before Edinburgh, there was always a danger that certain governments would succeed in chipping away at the *acquis communautaire*. This did not happen. The UK's list of over 70 measures of EC law to revise or repeal was dismissed. In place, (and emphasising the Commission's retained sole right of initiative) the Commission's list of over 20 was adopted as an example of what the modern EC should try to avoid. Some of those measures are deeply obscure; others are draft measures already blocked in the EC legislative processes. The Commission would have us believe that many of these now proscribed measures were brought forward in the first instance against its own better judgement following a request from member governments or from commercial or other lobbies.

The Commission proposes to withdraw (after Parliamentary consultation) 14 measures "not fully warranted in terms either of value added by Community action or of comparative efficiency in relation to other possibilities of action in the national or international contexts". It also proposes to amend six proposals that "go into excessive detail in relation to the objective pursued". It promises to re-examine certain technical, environmental and social policy directives with a view to simplification along the lines of mutual recognition of minimum standards, fair competition and freedom of movement. Finally, the Commission is abandoning preparatory work on a number of minor matters including the regulation of gambling and the harmonization of nuts and bolts. And it intends to use its monopoly of initiative to refuse requests from governments and the Parliament to draft new laws as well as to resist any unsuitable amendments.

The *Edinburgh Annex* also discusses the question of open government. The conclusions fall short of opening up the actual law-making of the Council to public scrutiny, but they were intended to make EC policy and legal processes less obscure. While avoiding doing anything to open up the procedures of the European Council, the leaders agreed to televise debates in the Council of Ministers on major issues of public interest, and to publish the voting record and explanation. Indeed, the incoming Danish President Elleman-Jensen quickly promised to hold its opening session of the General Council in front of the cameras. (He did — an anticlimax as a TV show, which the Belgian presidency is not repeating. The democratic campaign, however, needs to target the *close* of Council meetings, when the voting is taking place, and to insist on the publication of the minutes of the Council when it is acting in its legislative capacity.) The Common Position of the Council under the Article 189b (Co-decision) and 189c (Cooperation) procedures will be published — thereby fulfilling a major demand of the European Parliament. Lip-service is paid again to the need to simplify and codify EC law.

Subsidiarity Contested

The result of the UK General Election in April 1992 disappointed those who hoped for institutional change at home. The Conservative Party fought the campaign against Scottish and Welsh devolution, and against federal European Union. Ministers resisted the notion that European integration could or should have significant effects on the British political system. While in favour of the completion of the Single Market programme, they were against further extension of EC competence into social or environmental policy. Despite their signature of the Maastricht Treaty, they remained unconvinced of the need for EMU. Broadly speaking, the Tories support the enlargement of the Community yet oppose its deepening. And at home, while they remain committed to a limited reform of local government, the Conservatives are against major decentralization of national government. They are opposed to an electoral system based on multimember regional constituencies. They are against a written constitution and a Bill of Rights.

Part Two of this book is a collection of essays and reports from contributors chosen for the variety of their views about the meaning of subsidiarity within contemporary Europe. In **Chapter 2, Michael Burgess** discusses why it is that, in the light of the history of British federalism and the proud civic traditions of the country, subsidiarity should now appear so novel and federalism so threatening. He traces the influences of British federalist thought, and recommends its reinstatement on these shores.

The re-election of the Conservatives suggests that prospects for a federal Britain in a federal Europe are indeed distant. Meanwhile, the economic recession and currency turbulence is worse than anticipated. And in ex-Yugoslavia the first real war on European soil since 1945 makes less confident assertions about the achievements of European integration in general and of the European Community in particular. Europe's prevailing climate of pessimism is hardly a propitious background for radical political change. In these circumstances a leading role has been played by the Commission of Jacques Delors in motivating the debate about subsidiarity.

On the eve of the Edinburgh European Council in December 1992 the Federal Trust invited some of the leading participants in the subsidiarity debate to a conference in London. One of the main speakers was **Anthony Cary** who, in **Chapter 3** below, explains why the Commission believes the question of subsidiarity to be so important, and describes how the Commission made its contribution to Edinburgh.

Regional Devolution

Despite the Commission's obvious reticence about the matter, it is arguable that a greater measure of decentralization within Britain would bring considerable economic and political benefits. The establishment of strong regional authorities in Britain working in partnership with local commerce, industry and the voluntary sector, and networked to other comparable regions throughout the Single Market, might not have revolutionary consequences. Most UK ministries already have large provincial departments; many public utilities such as transport, health, water and broadcasting are already regionalised; the social partners and most NGOs have strong subnational branches.

In **Chapter 4, Alan Trench** argues that the growing federal element in the European Community does have a direct impact upon the internal disposition of its Member States, and analyses some of the legal complexities surrounding the application of subsidiarity in the United Kingdom.

Recent economic and political decentralization in most EC member states contrasts with the UK experience. The debate on subsidiarity in Britain benefits from comparison of the UK's internal disposition with that of its EC partners. The federalisation of Belgium, the reform of provincial and local government in the Netherlands, and the creation of autonomous government in Spain provide instructive case studies — as does the continuing debate between the Länder and Federal Government about the constitutional implications for Germany of the Maastricht Treaty. Italy, where the centralist unity of the Republic is contested by strong 'pro-European' regionalist forces, finds itself tottering like Britain between the inner core and the periphery of the Community. Even France, whose centralized structure of government used to resemble most nearly the UK's, has undergone substantial regionalization in recent years. This process, which resurrects some of the historical debate between the Girondins and Jacobins, is continuing.[14]

In **Chapter 5** we report these mainland comparisons as they were examined at the Federal Trust conference in December 1992. **Annemie Neyts** gives a critical review of Belgium's current reforms from her position as a national MP. **Carles Gasoliba**, a Catalan MEP, has a more optimistic analysis of the effect of EC subsidiarity on the internal disposition of Member States. **Otto Schmuck** explains the role of the Länder in the Bundesrat and draws some lessons for EC federalism from the German experience. **Paul Bongers** and **John Chatfield** review the experience of regional and local government representation in the EC before Maastricht, and look forward to the work of the Committee of the Regions. The summary of all these arguments is that the autonomous behaviour of regional and local government in the EC postulates already the formation of federal European Union. Subnational government is developing intra-Community connections, and both local and regional authorities are already making a contribution to building democracy in the EC.

Some of the most dramatic consequences of the 1992 general election were felt in Scotland. In March 1989 a Scottish Constitutional Convention had declared *A Claim of Right for Scotland* asserting the sovereign right of the Scottish people to determine their own form of government. The Convention produced formal proposals in November 1990 comprising, principally, the re-establishment of a Scottish Parliament elected by proportional representation as a first and immediate step towards a federal Britain. That the Convention opposed outright independence provoked the opposition of the Scottish National Party, and the Conservatives refused to participate from the outset. But the representative capability of the Convention was significant nevertheless, with senior Labour and Liberal Democrat politicians sitting alongside representatives of the churches, universities, trade and industry. However, despite the fact that in the 1992 general election nearly 75% of the Scottish electorate voted for the political parties of constitutional change (including the SNP), the Tory victory in England meant the 1707 Act of Union remains intact.

The Scottish Convention attracted curiously little publicity in the rest of Britain — either when it seemed to many Scots unstoppable or when it fell into disrepair. Nevertheless, Scotland's relations with Westminster remain a problem and an oddity — where else does a separate administration and legal system exist without a subsidiary government? There are analogies to be drawn between Scotland and the European Community, which also lacks a fully-fledged system of parliamentary government. What is clear, too, is that the growing importance of the EC presents a political as well as an economic opportunity for Scottish self-assertion.

In **Chapter 6**, 15 years after the last devolution legislation, **David Millar** and **Drew Scott** contribute their analysis of subsidiarity as a procedural and a substantive phenomenon. They draw conclusions for Scotland, and consider what the future prospects now may be for Home Rule. We also reproduce the debate from the Trust's London conference among three leading Scottish MPs: **Alex Salmond** for the SNP, **Henry McLeish** for Labour and **Jim Wallace** for the Liberal Democrats.

As far as the English regions are concerned, we may speculate on whether the present electoral system which tends to divide a mainly Tory South from the Labour North may be regarded as definitive, or whether a system of multimember constituencies where seats won at Westminster broadly matched the votes cast at elections would not provide for a clearer articulation of legitimate local, regional and party interests.

Local Government Reform
That there will be no regionalist devolution in Britain adds to the importance of the first structural reform of local government for a quarter of a century. This reform was promised by the government before the general election, and has

been set in train since. It follows many years of central government measures to restrict the autonomy of local government to raise and spend money, to build and own houses, to run transport services and to control education policy. Compulsory competitive tendering has opened up services to private operators that were for many years exclusive municipal concerns. School management of staff, finance and the curriculum is being taken out of the hands of local education authorities. Local government representatives no longer play the principal role in managing the National Health Service, and retain only a minimal one in Police affairs. The changes from the rates to the poll tax and now to the Council Tax, whatever their intrinsic merits, have been enormously costly and time-consuming for local government.

After a decade of centralization, shrinkage and falling morale it may have come as something of a relief to local councillors and officers that reform of the structure of local government, however limited, is now underway. The government is to allow the replacement of the existing two-tier system of local government with unitary authorities. It is likely that this change will contribute to the efficiency and accountability of councils. However, there will be no reform of the electoral system and certainly no significant reverse of the Conservatives' recent campaign to limit the powers and independence of local government in Britain. Moreover, with tight control of national public expenditure a lynch pin of the government's anti-inflation strategy, there will be no significant expansion of local revenue either.

The audience at the Trust's conference in December 1992 witnessed a vigorous debate between three leading English councillors, **Elgar Jenkins** for the Conservatives, **Jeremy Beecham** for Labour and **Andrew Stunell** for the Liberal Democrats. We reproduce their contributions in **Chapter 7**, preceded by an explanation by **Malcolm Grant** of the approach and prospects of the Banham Commission. We also reproduce in **Appendix Two** extracts from the Council of Europe's *Charter of Local Self-Government*, which the British government has refused to ratify and the EC has yet to sign.

Deepening EC Government

The completion of the Single Market now presents the EC with the complex problem of its economic and political management, and its legal enforcement. The Commission, especially in its communication of October 1992, has suggested the possibility of a large-scale administrative decentralization of its functions to national and subnational authorities. The problem of overload of comparatively mundane work is shared by the Commission with the European Court and Court of First Instance at Luxembourg. Such decentralization presupposes that low-level tribunals and local government would always be capable of enforcing EC law in a correct manner — possibly a wrong assumption at this stage of the Community's development. One solution, floated tentatively by the Commission, is for teams of national civil servants to monitor the implementation of EC law in countries other than their own. This already works in a limited way in the steel and fishery industries, but the prospect of foreign Euro-prefects roaming the byways of public administration is one for the most careful consideration.

Nevertheless, subnational public authorities have been affected by the EC's gradual liberalization of public procurement since 1971, and have since become an important agency for the implementation of EC law and policy in a wide range of areas, including health and safety at work, technical standardisation and environmental policy. Subnational government is also a vigorous supplicant for EC grant-aid for transport infrastructure, job creation, vocational training and industrial regeneration. This is especially so in the peripheral regions of the Community, of which the UK has many. A particular and well-known problem is that the UK Treasury did not accept the principle that EC funds should not be substituted for existing national public expenditure but be additional to it. This raised fundamental questions about the UK's commitment to the Community's system of 'own resources', but also cast doubt on the ability of the Commission to foster in the UK viable partnerships with regional and local development agencies or enterprises. In recent months, the Department of Trade and Industry has claimed that the quarrel over 'additionality' is now resolved to the satisfaction of both the Treasury and the Commission. Local authorities will watch developments closely, assisted by more information from the Commission. The more open supranational government, the more accountable subnational spending. The issue of additionality will surely be raised at an early meeting of the new Committee of the Regions.

The Treaty of Maastricht (Articles 198a,b,c) will establish an advisory Committee of the Regions. Although based upon the none too happy precedent of the Economic and Social Committee, with which it is to share an administrative budget, the Regional Committee is soon likely to outstrip ECOSOC in importance. The Committee will be consulted on culture (Article 128), on economic and social cohesion (Article 130b) and over the structural funds (Article 130e) and when the Commission or Council so decides. It can also initiate its own Opinions. The Committee of the Regions reinforces the development, in the name of EC cohesion, of a network of direct relationships between the subnational and supranational authorities which may threaten to by-pass and even subvert national control of local economic and social affairs. In the course of the passage of the Maastricht Bill the government conceded that UK members would all be local government councillors, thereby satisfying the demands made by the local government representatives at the Federal Trust conference in December. The local authority associations have now submitted nominations to the government. However, the Committee may still be thwarted by the variable calibre and capability of those appointed to it from across the Community. The prospect of the Chairman of Huntingdonshire District Council sitting between the Prime Ministers of Bavaria and Catalonia is, to say the least, diverting.

Widening EC Government
The application of subsidiarity poses legitimate questions about the widening scope of EC government. We have already noted that subsidiarity does not in itself attribute competences to any level of government but merely interprets

how such powers, bestowed by Treaty, should be exercised by the appropriate level of government. Article 3b, as we have seen, distinguishes between the application of subsidiarity over the EC's exclusive and shared competences. The Commission, for obvious reasons, insists on the integrity of the Community's exclusive competences. In its October 1992 memorandum on subsidiarity the Commission spelled out, possibly for the first time, what it deems these to be. At the heart of the Community's exclusive competence — that is, where Member State action is precluded — is Article 8a, added by the Single Act, which establishes the freedom of movement of goods, services and people. Related to the organization and protection of the internal market are the common commercial policy (Article 113), and the main features of transport, fishery, agriculture and competition policy. In Maastricht, of course, there is also the prospective exclusive competence to control the single currency.

The difficulties, however, in demarcating in practice the sharing of power between Community and national authorities may make it impossible to write down these exclusive competences in the proposed Interinstitutional Agreement. If that, as has been proposed, were even attempted, the Court of Justice would need to become directly involved in the formulation of the Agreement — a precedent which the Court might be very wise to avoid entirely.

At any rate, it is within the expanding area of shared or parallel competence that most scope for disagreement arises. The Treaty of Maastricht extends the shared competences of the EC to consumer protection (Article 129a), public health (Article 129), and culture (Article 128) — for regional and local government all highly significant areas — as well as strengthening the EC's environment portfolio (Article 130r,s,t). Article 3 of the Treaty admits the possibility of EC action in the fields of education, energy, tourism and civil protection — and doubtless these topics will appear on the agenda of the next IGC in 1996. The Community's incursion into cultural policy could have far-reaching implications for subnational ethnic and linguistic minorities. EC initiatives in the field of civic and language education and in broadcasting have already proved controversial, and are destined always to be so — and in most Member States, subnational authorities are directly involved in these controversies. The possibility of drastic action by the EC in these more peripheral areas of European integration should not be exaggerated, however. The Maastricht Treaty explicitly proscribes Commission-propelled harmonization measures, and the EC is most likely to move forward by mutual recognition and by voluntary cooperation.

Moreover, in many ways Maastricht simply writes down what has been happening anyway — Lord Mackenzie-Stuart has called it a "driving-mirror" Treaty. The incremental growth in the EC's exercise of competences has been steady, especially in the field of industrial policy. First the Single Act and now Maastricht have established a solid legal base for actions undertaken by the Community either under Article 235 or somewhat tangentially under single market or health and safety clauses. Under the terms of Maastricht there are few specifically brand new competences granted the EC — visas are perhaps the most important. Moreover, in these policy areas the powers given to the Commission and Parliament are strictly limited. Even under the terms of the contentious Social Protocol, the EC is explicitly precluded from making legislation on wages, strikes or union membership, and the Council has to act unanimously in the field of social security. The main thrust of the Agreement from which the UK is opting-out concerns physical working conditions, equality between men and women, and consultation of workers.

The UK's official expectation is that subsidiarity will curb the centralizing and busybody tendencies of the Community. The truth is, however, that subsidiarity cuts both ways. Its application can enforce action to be taken either at EC level or at national level. It can also be flexible, allowing powers to fluctuate according to circumstances. In an oil supply crisis, for example, it might be necessary for a temporary transfer of powers to enable intervention at the EC level. The British government is quite as active as any of its partners in promoting EC action that it sees to be to its advantage. In the Maastricht IGC it was even a strong advocate of giving the Court of Justice powers to penalize errant Member States for chronic non-compliance with EC law. It is ironic to hear the British government's political attacks on the power of the EC institutions and several contradictions flow from them. We have already referred to the dispute over the application of EC rules in the matter of additionality. It is also contradictory for the UK government to be seeking, on the one hand, to enforce EC rules about how often Spanish sheep are watered by Spaniards on the way to their local abattoir, and, on the other, opposing the incursion of EC environmental regulations at Twyford Down or Oxleas Wood. Worse, Britain continues to oppose the Commission's energy/CO_2 tax on the grounds of subsidiarity. This implies that one Member State could go on polluting others while reaping a fiscal advantage. All EC governments, of course, can apply double standards, but such behaviour from the UK does cast the British government's obsession with the ogre of the centralized superstate in a cold light. It also makes the Commission's job unenviable.

It is not, perhaps, the extent of the competences of the European Community, which are wide and flexible, that worry people as much as its powers, which are strong but obscure. The EC's own Barometer surveys of public opinion show firm support for central control of reasonable things, such as the environment and even defence. But the dimension of EC government, and its distance from ordinary people clearly provoke feelings of apprehension and antagonism. As we know, popular perception of 'Brussels' — often fed shamelessly by national politicians who should know better — is of a monster bureaucracy producing tidal waves of regulations governing the minutiae of daily life. In short, people tend to see the European Community as big, bossy and vaguely corrupt. But the fact of the matter is that the EC institutions, particularly but not only the Commission, are too weak not too strong. The variable reputation of the EC bureaucracy has much to do with a lack of financial and management resources at the centre and the uneven way in which policy is delivered by national and subnational agents. Politically, the central institutions are regularly blown off course by intervention from narrow national forces or by overweening lobby groups. Administratively, the EC institutions are often let down by national governments who deploy either excessive zeal or deplorable laxity in the execution of policy. The British government, in particular, has acquired a reputation for officiousness in turning EC directives into national practice.

We have discussed above the possibility of a more systematic decentralization, according to federalist principles, of the management and administration of the internal market. Clearly a prerequisite of such a strategy is the more uniform application of EC law across and within all Member States. An additional measure may be to disperse some of the activities of the institutions geographically across the Community. This could be achieved were a reduction in national jealousies to allow decisions to be taken about the siting of the proposed Environment Agency and other EC bodies. Another option is to pursue the strategy of transparent or open government suggested by adoption of the principle of subsidiarity. Above all, however, it is necessary to keep the dimension of EC government as small, and the force of its regulations as light as is consistent with technical efficiency. This may be an argument for keeping the EC budget a modest size, and for pushing spending power downwards as much as possible to the lower levels of regional and municipal government. In addition priority may be given to the rise of European Community citizenship. None of these options, it should be added, are unproblematical. None are exclusive. All have significant implications for the future development of the Community.

The European Citizen-Elector

As subsidiarity in its doctrinal context elevates the individual in society, one of the most important federalist features of the Maastricht Treaty is the creation of the political citizenship of the European Community. Certainly the Treaty attaches few civic rights and duties to the new-born creature, but the potential for enhancing them in the future is strong. European citizenship, true to the spirit of subsidiarity, is to complement but not supplant existing nationality. Of most significance is Article 8b of Maastricht which gives EC citizens the right to participate in municipal and European elections wherever they may live. This practical manifestation of common citizenship reinforces the need for provincial and local government to have improved access to the legal and political processes of the EC.

Another innovation (Article 8d) is the establishment of an EC Ombudsman to whom citizens will be able to take complaints of maladministration by EC institutions. Failure by the Commission to enforce additionality in the expenditure of EC structural funds would be an obvious example of a legitimate grievance. The setting up of the office of Ombudsman is another item for inclusion in the problematical Interinstitutional Agreement.

Nevertheless, it is as a symbol of popular sovereignty that European citizenship is most significant. Citizenship strengthens the representative capability of the

European Parliament, which will be greatly enhanced by being regarded as the repository of the pooled sovereignty of the people of Europe, just as the Council is seen as the repository of the pooled sovereignty of the states. The development of transnational political parties, under Article 138a of the Treaty, in order to articulate the political will of the citizen-elector will further enhance the Parliament — as would the establishment of a uniform electoral procedure under Article 138(3). In mainland Europe the republican tradition of popular sovereignty is stronger than in the British Isles — except in Scotland, where it was subordinated to the Westminster Parliament nearly 200 years ago. But, with the assistance of European civic education, the relative novelty of an advanced political citizenship should prove no impediment to its acceptance by pragmatic British people.

Subsidiarity in Practice

The Commission emerged from the Edinburgh Council reassured. Early in 1993 the Secretary-General of the Commission issued a set of seven questions to his staff which he invited them to answer when proposing new draft legislation. This practice is designed to internalize the 'subsidiarity test' within the Commission in the hope that clashes with the Council can be avoided. France and the UK are nevertheless preparing a new list of over 20 pieces of current EC legislation which they will ask the Commission to table for amendment or withdrawal. This list is thought to include the drinking water quality Directive. The Commission is still working on its own list, which may or may not coincide — as well as unilaterally withdrawing about 100 pieces of draft legislation in a separate, but associated, "house-cleaning exercise". Unfortunately, this Federal Trust Report is published before the completion of these exercises towards the end of 1993, but they promise to comprise the first real interinstitutional test of subsidiarity in practice.

In his annual 1993 report to the Parliament, Delors set great store on his "watchwords" of "democracy, subsidiarity and transparency".[15] He never ceased to be amazed, he said, how "some Member States" could be so hypocritical about the EC's democratic deficit. Pledging himself to a "crusade for democracy", the President added that "had the 1991 IGC accepted the Commission's idea, backed by Parliament, of a hierarchy of norms, the subsidiarity principle could have been applied more rationally without raising the fears that some of you share about a watering-down of the Community". During 1993, the Commission has put much effort into fleshing out its commitment to open government, and now has a self-confident policy on the dissemination of internal documents to the public, media and special interest groups which puts any national government to shame.[16]

Subsidiarity and transparency in practice bite as much on member governments as on the Commission, particularly in the management of the Single Market. In October 1992 Peter Sutherland completed a substantial report for the Commission on the management of the Single Market.[17] To establish mutual trust between member governments and conformity between national courts, Sutherland said that Member States needed to learn to 'work with the grain' of the Community — and vice versa. Business needed reassurance that subsidiarity would not lead to the erection of new barriers to free trade. EC measures should conform with the five criteria of need, effectiveness, proportionality, consistency and communication. As Anthony Cary foresees in Chapter 3, the Commission brought forward proposals to amend the 1983 Directive 189/EEC on the exchange of information about the standardization of technical barriers to trade, the purpose of which is to put an end to the spurious use by some Member States of national health and environmental regulations as a means of protection. Under the revised Directive EC governments would be obliged to provide fuller and franker information to each other and to the Commission about their own technical standards.[18]

Subsidiarity has, too, invaded the Council of Ministers. At Maastricht it was forced by the Germans (overcoming specifically Spanish opposition) to modify Article 146 to allow for ministerial representation in the Council from non-national — that is, regional — governments. This change, although discreet, is potentially highly significant for the growth of autonomous subnational government in the Community. A year later, at Edinburgh, the Council was for the first time forced to expose itself in some measure to the public gaze. Parliaments and press should in future learn much more about ministerial behaviour in the Council. However, the more liberal atmosphere prevailing has not yet resulted in the conclusion of the important new Interinstitutional Agreement on subsidiarity. That in 1993/94 there are in succession the three Council presidential terms of Denmark, Belgium and Greece is a complicating factor. Denmark was preoccupied not only with its second referendum but also with a change of government. Belgium, as we see below in Chapter 5, is in the middle of its own complex transition to federation, and may find the assertion of regional interests at EC level an additional difficulty. To conclude the Interinstitutional Agreement before the Committee of the Regions is set up may be tempting. Yet to delay until the next Greek presidency may be disastrous. In Greece subsidiarity is an unorthodox concept.

The Court of Justice, meanwhile, has the prospect of an ever-increasing workload when litigation alleging a breach of subsidiarity arises. Moreover, it will now have to take the Maastricht version of subsidiarity into account when it takes action under Article 173 to review the legality of EC acts. Perhaps the novelty of this should not be exaggerated: the Court has for several years stressed the need for proportionality between the intensity of EC law and the gravity of the case at issue. But the Maastricht Treaty has rendered subsidiarity firmly justiciable, and the European Court must prepare to treat itself and look forward to being treated by others as the supreme court of the European federation. Such, indeed, is the experience of the USA, where subsidiarity is a constant item of litigation — either because or in spite of the fact that the US Constitution delineates far more specifically than the EC Treaties what powers should by exercised by whom and at which level. In any case, the *Edinburgh Annex* promises to be a key piece of evidence in judgements about the meaning of Article 3b, which one engaged lawyer has called "good propaganda but bad law".[19]

The UK government has continued to assert that national action will be the rule and Community action the exception — a strategy of "minimum interference" (according to Douglas Hurd) and of "national precedence" (according to John Major).[20] The Tory MP David Howell, chairman of the influential Commons Foreign Affairs Committee, says that subsidiarity "in fact means that the centre is subordinate".[21] Study of the *Edinburgh Annex*, however, suggests these to be dubious assumptions. Immediately, in January 1993, for example, the European Parliament used the Edinburgh definition to call for a stronger, if more transparent, common environment policy, enforced by tougher action at EC level. (It is interesting to recall that Article 130R(4) of the Single Act states that the EC shall "take action relating to the environment to the extent to which the [Treaty] objectives can be attained better at Community level than at the level of the individual Member States".) Certainly, the European Court of Justice seems to be highly sensitive to any accusation of political adventurism. Could there ever be circumstances where a bold Court at Luxembourg would overturn a decisive Parliament at Strasbourg — especially one backed by the green lobby?

What seems more likely is that subsidiarity litigation will be generated by autonomous regional governments in Germany or Spain, and that judgements by the Court will have a side effect upon the operation of EC policy in all Member States no matter how centralized they themselves may now be. Indeed, the doctrine of 'national precedence' is likely to be whittled away from below in various ways by increasingly assertive regional and local government. European citizenship, the Committee of the Regions and the operation of the Single Market will combine to create the rationale and opportunity for active participation by subnational government in the supranational legal and political processes. Whenever the Community achieves its Maastricht objective of EMU, the competitive performance of regions within the integrated European economy may be determined by their political clout. Old-fashioned, centralist Member States that try to suppress regional autonomy — for example, in exploiting comparative advantages in the Ecu bond market — may lose out on investment. The UK government, for domestic and historic reasons, is working against this regionalist trend. But whether London can hold out for ever against domestic devolution must be questionable — especially if the government continues to emphasize the devolving charms of subsidiarity.

There is certainly evidence of discomfort in government circles about the devolution thesis. On his return from the Lisbon summit, John Major told the House of Commons that it was "perfectly clear that the principle of devolving — 'subsidiarity' is, we can all agree, an ugly word — means ensuring that we have a less intrusive Community and making sure that as much as is appropriate is done at the national rather than the European level".[22] Douglas Hurd, however, told MPs that subsidiarity "has nothing to do with devolution. It is actually common sense".[23]

The Commons Foreign Affairs Committee has taken a tentative view about how subsidiarity works in practice. It identified two approaches. First, subsidiarity "could form the basis of a more precise distribution of powers between the centre (either the Community itself, or ministers acting intergovernmentally), national governments and (in the eyes of some, particularly in countries with a more developed system of regional government) regional authorities". Second, national parliaments could be given the "power to veto central intervention if they considered that it would not enhance the achievement of the desired objectives". Or national parliaments could be given a "more specific role in the legislative process of the Community". The MPs remain dissatisfied about subsidiarity after Maastricht and Edinburgh, and call on the 1996 IGC to "entrench subsidiarity and restrain the growth of central power in the Community".[24] 'Entrench' implies a federal constitutional settlement. Is this the 'common sense' solution?

Jacques Delors, although clear about the moral requirements which underlie subsidiarity, has described it as a 'common sense principle' on a number of occasions. Sir Leon Brittan, who sees EMU as a classic example of subsidiarity, has called it both "a guiding political principle and a legal constraint", and seems to sympathise more with the approach of Valéry Giscard d'Estaing.[25]

What is subsidiarity?
Four things at least are clear about subsidiarity. First, whatever it is, it will always be in danger of over-simplification. Second, it has already changed the psychology of the Community. Third, it cannot be relied upon to stop European unification: it can be a centralizing as well as a decentralizing force. Fourth, it is not a formula producing mathematically correct answers to Europe's permanent dilemma of what powers should be exercised by whom and where. So what is it?

Subsidiarity is the principle that informs the development of European federal democracy. By 'federal' we mean the dispersal of powers between separate but coordinated democratic authorities. The European Community is a virtual federation of Member States.[26] The Community is not subordinate to the national authorities, but it is subsidiary or auxiliary. It is not a substitute for Member States but a supplement to them. Residual power lies not with the Community but with Member States, as in all federal republics.

Subsidiarity means that important powers — for example, citizenship, the internal market, external trade, competition policy, the protection of the environment, the control of money, and, ultimately, defence policy — can be transferred logically to a federal government at the European level. How many powers are transferred eventually will determine whether the existing European

Community becomes a fully-fledged federal state of Europe (much like the USA) or remains a federal Union of European States and Peoples (quite like nowhere else).

No matter what powers are pooled, however, the ensuing common policies need not be run entirely from Brussels, and in most cases the Community devolves the administration of policy on to lower tiers of government. National governments act as the agents of Community policy in most areas. Subnational government also takes on an increasing number of duties on behalf of the Community. In those Member States that are themselves federated residual power lies with the subnational authorities. German Basic Law (Article 30), for example, gives to the Länder the "exercise of the powers and functions of government". The Tenth Amendment to the Constitutions of the USA says that powers "not delegated to the United States by the Constitution, nor prohibited by it to the States, are reserved to the States respectively, or to the people". In other words, the German Länder and the American States, and not their federal governments in Bonn and Washington, remain generally competent. By contrast, in the United Kingdom all notional sovereignty and practical power resides with the Crown in Parliament at Westminster — in other words, with the British Government. The UK is now the most centralized unitary state in the EC, and Whitehall is subsidiary to nowhere.

The application of the federalist principle of subsidiarity is only possible within a federal system. Therefore subsidiarity can work within the European Community but not within the United Kingdom.

What *could* happen within the UK is a lot more decentralization of government ministries and agencies, and delegation of more power to local government. But under the present British constitution, power can only be devolved upon subnational or supranational authorities by the UK Parliament. Westminster can lend, loan, share or pool its sovereignty, but cannot abolish it. However much British sovereignty is diminished, it remains indestructible. So the UK Parliament could one day secede unilaterally from the European Union, but Scotland could not secede lawfully from the British Union without the consent of the Westminster Parliament — unless, of course, the UK had in the meantime transformed itself into a constitutional federation.

All this makes the constitutional problem of EC membership so thorny in Britain. The British predicament may excuse some of the confusion caused by the introduction of the concept of subsidiarity. Much UK media comment, fed by Westminster, has talked of subsidiarity as if it were a revolutionary notion designed to return to unfettered national jurisdiction major parts of government. Such talk disregards the continuing obligation under the Treaty to uphold the common market and respect the corpus of the *acquis communautaire*. The repeal of hectares of EC legislation looks most improbable, and would, in any case, have to run the gauntlet not only of the Council and Commission but also of the out-of-the-closet federalist majority in the European Parliament. It is quite clear that no UK government would find allies in the Community if it were systematically to deploy subsidiarity as a subversive weapon.

In the constitutional development of the European Community, nevertheless, subsidiarity promises to be an abiding force subject to perpetual redefinition. As the dimension of European integration increases, the profile of what Giscard d'Estaing has called "the federal pact" will become sharper. In this configuration there may well be a case for a more prominent role for national parliaments. (This, indeed, is the subject of a new Federal Trust enquiry.) The Commission has promised to issue Green Papers at the preparatory stage of the formulation of its proposals, and national parliaments will be at liberty to discuss them, to invite the Commission to answer questions and to express opinions. Furthermore, if the EC adopts the hierarchy of norms proposal at the 1996 IGC, there will be European framework acts requiring detailed implementation by national parliaments.

To make the most of these and other opportunities to influence the development of the Community, the British Parliament would be wise soon to jettison its bizarre hang-up about federalism. Doubtless, British politicians could make a positive contribution to European integration if they stopped talking in riddles about it. Subsidiarity, after all, requires self-restraint and scrutiny at the national as well as Community level. It is not impossible that political and institutional reforms within other Member States hold out some lessons for Britain about how to adapt to the pressure of continuing European integration. Certainly, there can be no question of any meaningful collaboration with other EC national parliaments until Westminster becomes less obsessional.

Contrary to the general perception of what was happening at Westminster, the recent and protracted Maastricht Bill was neither ratifying the Treaty on European Union (which the government did) nor ceding parliamentary sovereignty (which nobody can do). In passing the European Communities (Amendment) Act 1993 Parliament was incorporating into UK domestic law the transfer and sharing of certain national powers with fellow Member States of the European Community. By legislating for European subsidiarity it was building the federal relationship for Britain in Europe.

---

[1] The history of subsidiarity and its place in federalist thought is discussed in Marc Wilke and Helen Wallace *Subsidiarity: Approaches to Power-sharing in the European Community* Royal Institute of International Affairs Discussion Paper 27 1990. See also Andrew Adonis and Andrew Tyrie *Subsidiarity: no panacea* European Policy Forum 1992
[2] EC Bulletin 6/89 1.1.11
[3] HC Debate Vol 210 col 986 2 July 1992 and Reports of the Foreign Affairs Committee *Europe After Maastricht* HC 223 I-II 1991-92; HC 205 1992-93; HC 642 I-II 1992-93. For a previous discussion of subsidiarity see *The Operation of the Single Act* HC 82 1989-90
[4] EC Bulletin Supplement 2/91 p81

[5] As above p122

[6] Article 235 is reprinted on p5

[7] The Dutch presidency of the IGC in the second half of 1992 supported the inclusion of the Parliament in the Article 235 procedure.

[8] EC Bulletin Supplement 1/92 p11

[9] HC Debate Vol 208 col 265-70 20 May 1992

[10] EC Bulletin 10/92 2.2.1

[11] This form of words was re-defined by the Luxembourg and Dutch presidencies of the IGC to read:-"La Communauté agit dans les limites des compétences qui lui sont conférées et des objectifs qui lui sont assignés par le présent traité. Dans les domaines qui ne relèvent pas de sa compétence exclusive, la Communauté n'intervient, conformément au principe de la subsidiarité, que si et dans la mesure où les objectifs qui lui sont assignés peuvent être mieux réalisés au niveau communautaire qu'au niveau des Etats membres oeuvrant isolément, en raison des dimensions ou des effets de l'action envisagée"

[12] OJ C 324 24 December 1990

[13] EP Document A3-163/90

[14] See JA Chandler ed *Local Government in Liberal Democracies* Routledge 1993; Christian Engel and Jef Van Ginderachter *Trends in Regional and Local Government in the European Community* TEPSA 1993; *The Structure of Local Government in the European Community* IULA 1987

[15] EC Bulletin Supplement 1/93 pp10-11

[16] See for example *Openness in the Community* COM(93) 258 final 2 June 1993

[17] SEC(92) 2277 2 December 1992

[18] OJ C 340 23 December 1992

[19] Leolin Price QC in Parliamentary Brief Vol 1 no 2 1992

[20] Douglas Hurd: Foreign Affairs Committee HC 642-II 1992-93 p87; John Major: Speech to Conservative Group for Europe 22 April 1993. See also Anthony Teasdale *Subsidiarity in Post-Maastricht Europe* in Political Quarterly April 1993

[21] HC Debate Vol 208 col 305 20 May 1992

[22] HC Debate Vol 210 col 588 29 June 1992

[23] Foreign Affairs Committee HC 223-II 1991-92

[24] HC 642-I pp xx & xxix

[25] Agence Europe No 5752 18 June 1992

[26] See John Pinder *The Community After Maastricht: how federal?* New European Quarterly Review vol 5 no 3 1993

- PART TWO -

CHAPTER TWO

The British Federal Tradition

by Michael Burgess

Unitary State - Myth or Reality
Among the many paradoxes which lie at the heart of the United Kingdom the phrase 'Unitary State' seems particularly perplexing. Scholars who have written recently about it seem to veer awkwardly between constitutional theory which is unequivocal and constitutional theory which is ambiguous. This is because although the United Kingdom is a state in terms of international law it nonetheless has no written constitution. As Richard Rose has argued, "the stateless and non-constitutional nature of government in the United Kingdom means that questions about its institutions and territorial extent are neither confronted nor resolved." [1] However he remains emphatic that "the United Kingdom meets the basic definitional criteria of a unitary state. The Crown in Parliament is the sole political authority, and its authority is formally unlimited". Authority in a unitary state, then is clearly undivided and where there appear to have been departures from this axiom they have been "more apparent than real". [2]

Vernon Bogdanor, in his *Devolution*, also acknowledged the highly centralised and "profoundly unitary nature of the United Kingdom, as expressed in the supremacy of Parliament", but he distinguished this from "the spirit in which this unitary state is administered". [3] Here centralisation as a force of habit rather than of ideology has permitted a wide diversity of political relationships:—

> "British politicians have rarely allowed a theory of government to prevent them from constructing new relationships, which, whatever the faults to be found in them by strict constitutionalists, nevertheless succeed in providing workable answers to practical problems". [4]

Rose and Bogdanor lead us inexorably to the conclusion that the United Kingdom is a unitary state without a unitary constitution. But the formal trappings of the unitary state have not in practice stifled every attempt to redefining relations between England and Scotland, Wales and Ireland during the last few centuries.

In his *Territory and Power in the United Kingdom*, Jim Bulpitt denies that the post-Union structure of government was unitary "in so far as that term has any meaning". His thesis emphasises the reluctance of the central authorities to interfere directly in the affairs of local communities and depicts a "peculiar structure of territorial politics ... characterized by a high degree of constitutional ambiguity". [5] In summary, then, the authority of the Crown in Parliament has remained largely intact. The United Kingdom developed as a unitary state in theory but both the instinct and the spirit of its practice have been intermittently imaginative and flexible. As Rose has remarked, the state was unitary but not uniform.[6] Hence in the absence of an overwhelming centralist ideology dedicated to cultural uniformity via a single integrated organisation, both the myth and the reality of the unitary state have been perpetuated in the United Kingdom — that intellectual puzzle.[7]

The Origins of the British Federal Tradition

Among those who study federal political thought and practice, it is common to regard British philosophical and political ideas on this subject as somehow 'empirical, pragmatic and instrumental'. It is certainly conceded that a basic philosophical corpus of thought lies at the root of this tradition, but it tends to be passed over in favour of the practical study of federal, or federal-type, structures. One unfortunate consequence of this neglect is to leave the impression that the philosophical origins of British federalism are so weak that they do not merit more than cursory attention. At best, the philosophical content of the British tradition of federalism is deemed to be implicit rather than explicit.

Since the modern federal idea owes nothing either to classical Greek or Middle Ages Italian political arrangements, it is in the gradual appearance of the elaborate 'social contract' theory of the seventeenth and eighteenth centuries that we must locate the origins of British federalism. In the great pantheon of English political thinkers who helped to shape the new philosophical climate in which old, encrusted ideas of authority and obligation were quickly discredited, the names of Thomas Hobbes, Algernon Sydney, John Locke and David Hume loom large. Political theorists trace a fairly consistent line of thought — grounded in social contract, natural rights, popular consent, the justification of resistance to authority, and utilitarianism — which brings into question the very essence of sovereign power.

Hobbes's *Leviathan* (1651) and Locke's *Treatise on Civil Government* (1690) both epitomise the shift from Absolutism and the Divine Right of Kings to the subversive ideas of consent — the notion of a compact or contract freely entered into — and limited government. It is important to note that none of these thinkers contributed directly to the modern federal idea, but they did create the fundamental philosophical basis upon which it could grow and develop. The importance of Rousseau and Montesquieu to the emergence of the modern federal idea should also be acknowledged here because their own philosophical impact upon the political environment of late eighteenth century America proved to be crucial. Montesquieu's influence is particularly significant because it was his interpretation of the English Constitution which the founders of the American Republic had before them, not as a blueprint to transplant to the New World, but as a guide to the strengths and weaknesses of governmental organisation.

In 1776, the year that the leading colonial revolutionaries drafted and issued the Declaration of Independence, it is clear that the underlying political theory in the American colonies was largely identical to that of seventeenth century England. In short, the philosophical environment was conducive to constitutional experimentation and political speculation. If we set the practical realities which confronted the American colonists against this changed philosophical background, it is easy to appreciate how far the 'Anglo-American' federal tradition emerged from the complex interaction of theory and practice. Both were necessary in the creation of the first modern federation.

After 1787 the American federal invention became the yardstick according to which later federal proposals were judged. The British, having reconciled themselves to the loss of the American colonies, became great exporters of the federal idea. But it is important to note that British federal ideas were shaped and moulded by the development of the British constitution as it worked in practice rather than as it was both intended and expected to operate in 1688. In other words, the evolution first of cabinet, and then prime ministerial, government reflected the fusion of legislative and executive powers instead of their anticipated separation. The shift of legitimate authority from the monarchy to parliament meant that executive power derived from parliament and that the constitution enshrined the 'sovereignty of parliament' rather than the American version which entrenched the 'sovereignty of the people' in the constitution.

This difference in constitutional meaning is fundamental and has had important consequences for the way in which the British have perceived and prescribed the federal model. Theirs, naturally, is a perception which is rooted in the British parliamentary tradition. Canada was the first example of the modern federal idea being put peacefully and voluntarily into practice in 1867 after the consolidation of the American innovation. But Canada did not follow the American model. The influence of British parliamentary practice together with the chastening experience of the American Civil War predisposed Canadians to seek the then novel variation of combining the federal principle with parliamentary government. And if many Canadian critics today have condemned this combination as inherently unworkable for the simple reason that the two principles are essentially incompatible, this has not deterred others from implementing it.

In the twentieth century it has been employed in many countries, but in a variety of different ways. The inherent flexibility of the model has been crucial to its success. Where there are, for example, socio-cultural cleavages which have acute political salience, as in Canada, India and Malaysia, the model has the capacity both for constitutional innovation and institutional adaptation designed to re-establish legitimacy, order and stability. But British federal perceptions have been influenced by more than just the nature of constitutional development. The British legal and parliamentary tradition, epitomised in the nineteenth century views of A.V. Dicey whose enormously influential *The Law and the Constitution* appeared in 1885, cannot but see federation as inherently weak. Dicey regarded it as rigid, conservative and inherently legalistic. The written constitution which it required necessarily enhanced the role of the judiciary and this collided head-on with the hallowed British political tradition of 'parliamentary sovereignty'. From this late nineteenth century perspective, federation was construed as justifiable only if there were no possibility of constructing the more complete union, namely, the unitary state.

We can see from this brief sketch outline that the origins of the British tradition of federalism stretch back at least to the seventeenth and eighteenth centuries, and that they incorporate the American colonial experience as a catalyst of political and constitutional experimentation. Indeed, it would be appropriate to emphasise the British imperial tradition in general as a broad framework within which the British themselves toyed intermittently with ideas of parliamentary reform and political reconstruction. In the nineteenth century, British imperial problems provoked a whole series of federalist responses and it is to these that we can now turn our attention.

Empire, Ireland and the Federal Idea, 1870-1918
The very existence of the British Empire prompted serious consideration of the federal idea. Adam Smith was the first to recommend it in his *Wealth of Nations* published in 1776. Representation of the American colonies in the British parliament in proportion to the contribution of American taxation, he argued, would facilitate a better balance of forces between the monarchical and the democratic aspects of political authority. The subsequent development of the colonial reform movement during the 1830s in Britain led directly to the granting of responsible government to many of the settled colonies in the 1840s and 1850s. This new British imperial relationship, which fostered local autonomy principally in the white self-governing colonies, gradually undermined old conceptions of empire and provoked a searching public debate about Britain's imperial future. The reappraisal of empire which had, in a sense, continued throughout the first half of the nineteenth century reached something of a climax during the late 1860s and marked a watershed in the history of the British federal tradition.

The mid-Victorian era witnessed a sudden surge in the popularity of the federal idea about 1870. If we focus sharply upon the period 1870-1918 the evidence for the rise of the federal idea in British politics is overwhelming. For nearly fifty years after 1870 the phrase 'Imperial Federation' was part and parcel of popular political discourse and served as a convenient rallying cry for those who sought a much more binding and regulated empire but who could not agree upon the details of how it should be achieved. In practice it was a useful mobilising ploy for the imperialism of consolidation rather than expansion, and it led to a host of constitutional reform proposals which sought to strengthen imperial ties. Most of those who sympathised with this vague ideal did not necessarily believe that the utilization of the federal principle meant superimposing on the empire the whole paraphernalia of a federal constitution analogous to that of the United States. Such activists who worked to this end were in a tiny minority. But this still left available a very extensive range of Empire federalist schemes which permitted numerous variations of the federal idea. Most of them were what we might today call 'federal instalments' and ranged from well-worn proposals for sending colonial MPs to Westminster to the creation of advisory bodies of colonial agents based in London to advise Parliament on colonial affairs.[8]

It is important to note that during these years the two dominant themes in British politics — Empire and Ireland — were interrelated in a close and complex fashion. This is why together they provided the main impetus for the nourishment of federal, and federal-type, solutions. The problem of Ireland could not be divorced from its imperial context. Hence federal constitutional reform within the United Kingdom was indissolubly linked to federal constitutional reform vis-à-vis the white self-governing empire.

Throughout the 1870s federalism, loosely referred to as 'imperial federation', was hotly debated both in the Royal Colonial Institute (RCI) and in the plethora of articles and essays which appeared in the mid-Victorian press and review literature.[9] In Parliament too, the federal idea began to be taken seriously. Indeed, its significance in British politics at this time was such that it was able to sustain a political movement created in 1884 and entitled the Imperial Federation League. Founded on 29 July 1884 at the Westminster Palace Hotel the new League sought both to publicise and to popularise the idea of 'imperial federation' and was committed to "secure by Federation the permanent unity of the Empire". It received its official public baptism on 18 November and under the leadership successively of W.B. Forster, Lord Rosebery and Lord Brassey was the most important public expression of closer imperial union until its abrupt collapse in December 1893.[10] Altogether thirty-one branches of the League were formed in England and Scotland during these years and membership hovered at around the figure of 2000. The membership size is, however, misleading. Since it included mainly important and influential public figures, drawn from the elites of British and colonial societies, it represented a potentially significant force for almost any cause it might promote. Its very existence was ample testimony to the strength and progress of the federal idea in the United Kingdom in the late-Victorian period.

The League's demise in 1893 occurred only after it had crossed the Rubicon by formulating a specific federal scheme for the Empire.[11] Gladstone's rejection of the League's federal plan was perhaps inevitable, but the pursuit of 'imperial federation' did not die with the disappearance of the League. Indeed, it was rekindled in 1909-10 when the Round Table movement was formed. Destined to dominate British intellectual thinking about Empire-Commonwealth relations until the early 1920s, the movement served as a crucial repository of imperial federationist ideas which represented a basic continuity of thought and action between the late nineteenth and early twentieth centuries in terms of the reorganisation of the British state.[12]

Imperial federation was the link which ran beneath the surface of the activities of public men like Lionel Curtis and Philip Kerr, later Lord Lothian, who were among the founders of the new political movement in Edwardian England. This connection was expressed by the nebulous phrase 'organic union' but it is clear that "the discovery of some form of federation which shall be at once effective and acceptable" was the main focus of their energies.[13] Their main strategy, like that of the Imperial Federation League, was to popularise the federal idea and to influence official thinking; but there the similarity ended. They avoided the mistake of their predecessors. Concentrating less on mass agitation than on influencing leadership, they recognised that popular support was valuable only after politicians had raise the issue. This, as Ged Martin observed, determined their tactics: "Major policy problems, like the role of India in a federal union, were thrashed out in secret memoranda. Lobbying was confined to the powerful".[14] And as the historian of the movement, John Kendle, remarked "the movement, particularly the London group, did have some influence in governmental circles in Great Britain and in the Dominions, not least because its members came from the affluent, the well-placed, the intellectual and generally the most acceptable members of society".[15]

If we turn to the specific question of Ireland during these years, there is plenty of evidence to demonstrate both the vitality and the visibility of federalism in the British political tradition. Federalism was advocated in the 1870s by Isaac Butt and his Home Rule Party, but its significance loomed much larger in the mid-1880s when Joseph Chamberlain first propounded it as the solution to the Irish problem. As one of the most famous and influential reform agitators of the late-Victorian era, Chamberlain was a consistent opponent of any home rule scheme which threatened the imperial connection, but the Birmingham Radical was certainly not averse to constitutional or other reforms which would keep Ireland in the Union. It is here that the federal idea assumed a growing importance in the Radical leader's mind.

His support for the federal solution to Irish home rule can be traced back at least to 1874 when he approved Isaac Butt's proposal called a 'federal arrangement' and it was firmly incorporated in the famous Radical Programme of 1885. Here the primary aim of a federal reorganisation of British government was the devolution of parliamentary business which would improve the efficiency of legislation by freeing the 'imperial parliament' to confine itself to foreign affairs, trade, defence and colonial matters. This fundamental rationale of federalism and what was later called 'Home Rule All Round' provides the explanatory background to Chamberlain's disruptive parliamentary behaviour in 1886. His somewhat sudden interventions for the federal cause during the epic debate on Gladstone's first Home Rule Bill in the House of Commons in April and June 1886 can be understood only if we recognise that the retention of elected Irish representatives at Westminster was the touchstone of his faith: if they remained then a federal home rule scheme for the United Kingdom was feasible.[16]

Gladstone's second Home Rule Bill successfully traversed the House of Commons in 1893 but was rejected by the House of Lords. However, the Irish question returned during 1912-14 to dominate British government and politics, threatening the survival of Asquith's Liberal government and dividing the Conservative Party along several lines of strategy and tactics.[17] The third Home Rule Bill received the royal assent in September 1914 but was held in abeyance for the duration of the war. In these troubled years the federal idea was prominent in the protracted discussions about Ireland's future and the Round Table Group played an important role in its reshaping and reappearance as 'Home Rule All Round'.[18]

In 1910 federal solutions were canvassed in the Constitutional Conference, assembled to resolve the conflict between the Commons and the Lords. Austen Chamberlain, a leading member of the Conservative Opposition, resurrected his father's old policies and became the leading exponent of federalism in the party and, later, in Lloyd George's Coalition Government in 1918. The growing significance of the federal idea in Unionist circles was clearly due to its perceived capacity to solve the Irish problem while maintaining the integrity of the Union, but support for it also spread to the Liberal Party. As First Lord of the Admiralty who had introduced the second reading of the Government of Ireland Bill in the House of Commons, the young Winston Churchill revealed his conversion to the federal cause in a major public speech during September 1912 when he urged his Dundee constituents to consider a federal United Kingdom. John Kendle noted that Churchill spoke speculatively and not as a Cabinet representative but his speech had "wide reverberations" and he "helped in making federalism a major talking-point once more in party intellectual circles; and it remained at the forefront of the political stage until the early summer of 1914".[19]

In 1914 the outbreak of war effectively halted the public debate about Ireland and wider constitutional reform for the United Kingdom. But it was back on the public policy agenda in 1918. According to Kendle, "it was only with the virtual breakdown of negotiations over the home rule question in early 1918 and the apparent need to introduce conscription in Ireland that federalism began to seem a reasonable alternative to many British politicians".[20] Federal schemes received wide coverage in the British press and figured prominently in both Scottish and Welsh home rule circles. Indeed, one estimate put the support for 'federalism for its own sake' at about 50 Unionists, 90 Liberals and an uncertain number of Labour MPs.[21] However, a personal survey conducted for Lloyd George in May 1918 to weigh the strength of the federalists put their numbers at around 340 MPs spanning virtually the entire party political spectrum. And on the Irish committee set up by the Prime Minister to draft a home rule bill acceptable to all interested groups, discussion and negotiation on political and financial issues alike took place "constantly within an ideological framework of federalism".[22]

It is clear that by April 1918 both Lloyd George and Austen Chamberlain were agreed upon a scheme of Irish home rule which would 'fit in with a Federal plan'; it would facilitate 'Home Rule All Round'. The Prime Minister, however, was exposed to conflicting views within the War Cabinet, and while it was true that opinion in the Irish Committee had hardened in the direction of a federal system, the War Cabinet was not disposed to embark upon a full-scale overhaul of the United Kingdom. The end of the War brought to a close perhaps the most heady period of public debate about constitutional reform in this country, and our brief survey of it confirms Bogdanor's assertion noted above that the unitary nature of the state has not prevented a wide diversity of political relationships from existing within the United Kingdom. It has also not deterred serious public consideration of the federal idea in British government and politics.

British Federal Ideas and European Unity
The federal idea did not peter out at the end of the First World War. The Speaker's Conference on Devolution, created in October 1919, ensured that reform of the constitutional structure of the United Kingdom remained at the forefront of British politics in the immediate post-war era. The aim of the Conference was not the discussion of general principle but "the consideration of practical schemes of devolution". Alluding to these in broad terms as 'Federal Devolution', this all-party conference of Lords and Commons reached agreement upon four out of five separate sections in the Report and recognised the federal principle underlying the division of powers between the UK Parliament and the subordinate regional parliaments which would be created. Indeed, as one expert commentator upon the Speaker's Conference wrote in 1926, "the result of this will be federalism in the broadest sense, for the common feature of all federal states is the division of power".[23]

The two most important changes which radically altered traditional British perceptions of the state and of its constitutional structure occurred between 1921 and 1931. The formal creation of Ulster and the Irish Free State in 1921 and the Statute of Westminster in 1931 both served to change Britain's legal and constitutional relations with Ireland and the Commonwealth in a manner which rendered the consideration of a federal solution impracticable and unnecessary. The white self-governing empire had gone and Ireland had been truncated. Federalism maintained only a very weak relevance to the new Irish problem and none at all to the Commonwealth.

Up until the 1930s the British federal tradition had been concerned with the various dimensions of domestic statecraft. British political and economic elites had looked upon the federal idea principally as means of reorganising and reconstructing the British imperial state. During the interwar years, however, the new constellation of power relations in Europe prompted a searching reappraisal of traditional British foreign policy. One consequence of Britain's changing relationship to Europe in the 1930s was the beginning of a new interest in the international character of federalism. The growing threat of war in Europe sparked a number of innovative public organisations into existence in Britain, the most important of which was the Federal Union. Formed in 1938 by a committed group of Oxford graduates, the new political movement was originally animated by the desire to prevent war. It came to propound federalism as a theory of political organisation and towards the end of the Second World War as a strategy for reconstruction both in Europe and throughout the world.[24]

As Walter Lipgens's account of its development demonstrates, the movement reached the peak of its effectiveness during 1940-41, "having grown with astonishing speed and produced an equally astonishing output of books and pamphlets".[25] If we consider that its active local organisations numbered just over 200 in February 1940 and that these had grown to 225 branches totalling 12,000 members by June 1940 we can appreciate once again just how far the federal idea had retained its vitality, resilience and relevance in British political life during the twentieth century. The significance of the Federal Union as a channel through which distinct *British* federal ideas made an important intellectual contribution to post-war European integration has at last been recognised.

The links between the 1930s and 1940s and the current debate about European Union in the 1990s are now firmly established. They originate in the pivotal role played by Altiero Spinelli in the cause of a closer, more binding Europe which he championed from about 1937 until his death in 1986.[26] Spinelli's impact upon the debate about Europe, especially in the 1980s, has been colossal. His activities as a member of the Commission of the European Community with responsibility for Industry, Research and Technology during 1970-76 and his crucial influence as a member of both the Italian and European Parliaments in the drive to achieve European Union in the early 1980s have combined to place him in a position alongside Jean Monnet as one of Europe's great architects. Spinelli made a large contribution to the political revitalisation of the EC in the early 1980s and launched the process in the European Parliament which culminated in 1984 in the European Union Treaty. Although itself not implemented by the Member States, it provided the impetus and furnished the context for the ratification of the Single European Act in 1987.

Spinelli's own contribution to the goal of European Union has a double significance. First, his political ideas about Europe were federal ideas and, secondly, these federal ideas were *British* federal ideas. Spinelli was particularly influenced by the federalist literature of Federal Union, and the views and arguments of Lord Lothian, Lionel Robbins and William Beveridge made a strong impression upon him.[27] These ideas proved to be both decisive and durable. In his autobiography the attraction of British federal ideas was lucidly explained:—

"Since I was seeking clarity and precision of thought my attention was not attracted by the nebulous, contorted and hardly coherent ideological federalism of the Proudhonian or Mazzinian type, which throve in France or in Italy, but by the polished, precise and anti-doctrinaire thought of the English federalists ... who proposed to transplant into Europe the great American political experience".[28]

Spinelli certainly read Lothian's *Pacifism is not enough* and Robbins's *The Economic Causes of War.* [29] In the following extract from an essay which he wrote in 1957 the impact of British federal ideas is reaffirmed:—

"We are used to thinking of the British as completely averse to any idea of federation, and they, themselves, seem to strengthen this impression by often repeating that this is ... very foreign to their method of thinking. ... This is actually not so, however. ... The idea that it is possible to bring about a supranational government by means other than conquest, ie. through free consent of states, and that it is possible to divide sovereignty, assigning portions of it to different organs of the government, is a typically Anglo-Saxon conception. ... We must conclude that the federal experience is very close to the British political spirit, and also that the British can easily understand the federal concept and its logical and economic implications. Another proof is seen in the federalist literature of the Federal Union, which is of first quality and even today superior to the average Continental literature on the subject, because of the coherence with which the problems are presented, the obstacles examined, and solutions proposed. It is interesting to note here that the most coherent federalist movement today is the Italian which has absorbed a great deal from the study of this English federalist literature". [30]

Spinelli's intellectual ideas were "rooted in English political culture". [31] The profile of Alterio Spinelli's political life and career demonstrates above all else the great significance of British federal ideas in the cause of European integration. It is, indeed, a long and quite remarkable progeniture and it reaffirms the substantive importance which we should attach to the British federal tradition.

This focus upon British federal ideas and European unity confirms that the historical shift from Empire and Ireland to Europe is at last complete. But it does not suggest the exhaustion of these ideas. On the contrary, the specifically British contribution to a 'European Union of federal type', as the European Parliament has recently described it, is today even more pertinent. [32] In the EC the word 'federal' is no longer taboo in political discourse, but it is vitally important that the public debate in the 1990s about the future of Europe takes place in an atmosphere which is conducive to constructive thought. In the UK a more general awareness of the British federal tradition and its peculiar contribution to European integration would assist towards this goal.

The British Federal Tradition Reinstated

This chapter argues that at the levels both of political ideas and political practice federalism should be firmly reinstated in the British political and constitutional tradition. The history and development of the United Kingdom suggest in the most practical way that federalism is more indigenous to British political culture than conventional wisdom would have us believe. For over a century Empire, Ireland and Europe have provided the framework for repeated attempts at institutional and constitutional reform and reconstruction of the British state. Federal ideas and proposals have manifested themselves sometimes clearly and sometimes in a very confused manner. They have occasionally been prominent and they have often been peremptorily dismissed. But it is equally clear that there exists a continuous unbroken tradition of federal ideas which have been perfectly rational, considered responses to the perceived defects and deficiencies of the British state itself.

In his classic work entitled *The Problem of Federalism* which first appeared in 1931, Sobei Mogi remarked that "we cannot fail to realise that the political organisation of Great Britain has taken the form of a self-governing community from the time of the early settlers". "Experience in local self-government", he added, "and the training given by parliamentary institutions, enlightened by the tolerant teaching of Protestantism and the growth of political philosophy, determined the essential features of federalism as developed by the people of Great Britain". [33] It is ironic, given this long experience of an essentially federal political culture, that the British have largely forgotten their past. It is time to reinstate it.

---

[1] R Rose *Understanding the United Kingdom* p48 London 1982

[2] As above p52

[3] V Bogdanor *Devolution* pp7-8 Oxford 1979

[4] As above p8

[5] J Bulpitt *Territory and Power in the United Kingdom* pp96-99 Manchester 1983

[6] Rose p54

[7] R Rose *The United Kingdom as an Intellectual Puzzle* in D Jeansch ed *The Politics of 'New Federalism'* pp21-34 Adelaide 1977

[8] For a detailed survey of these schemes see SC Cheng *Schemes for the Federation of the British Empire* London 1931 & G Martin *Empire federalism and Imperial Parliamentary Union 1820-1970* in The Historical Journal vol XVI I pp65-72

[9] See T Reese *The History of the Royal Commonwealth Society, 1866-1966* London 1966

[10] For an explanation of the League's appearance in 1884 see M Burgess *Forgotten Centenary: The formation of the Imperial Federation League in Great Britain, 1884* in The Round Table vol 289 January 1984.

[11] See M Burgess *The Federal Plan of the Imperial Federation League 1892* in A Bosco ed *The Federal Idea: The History of Federalism from the Enlightenment to 1945* vol 1 pp139-153 London 1991

[12] See J Kendle *The Round Table Movement and Imperial Union* Toronto 1975

[13] Kendle p64. On Lothian see JRM Butler *Lord Lothian (Philip Kerr), 1882-1940* London 1960.

[14] G Martin *The Idea of Imperial Federation* in R Hyam and G Martin *Reappraisals in British Imperial History* p133 London 1975

[15] Kendle p305

[16] See S Gwynn and G Tuckwell *The Life of the Rt Hon Sir Charles Dilke* vol 2 pp199-201 & p217 London 1917

[17] See R Murphy *Faction in the Conservative Party and the Home Rule Crisis, 1912-1914* in

History vol 71 1966 pp222-234

[18] See J Kendle *The Round Table Movement and Home Rule* in The Historical Journal vol 11-2 pp332-353 1966

[19] Kendle *The Round Table Movement* p349

[20] J Kendle *Federalism and the Irish Problem in 1918* in History vol 56 p207 1971

[21] As above pp213-214

[22] As above pp217 & 222

[23] See WH Chaio *Devolution in Great Britain* pp184 & 190 New York 1926. See also the brief description in JC Banks *Federal Britain?* London 1971 pp82-85

[24] See J Pinder & R Mayne *Federal Union: The Pioneers* London 1990

[25] W Lipgens *A History of European Integration 1945-47* vol 1 p142 Oxford 1982

[26] For a detailed analysis of the intellectual origins of Spinelli's political ideas see M Burgess *Altiero Spinelli Federalism and the EUI* in J. Lodge ed *European Union: The European Community in Search of a Future* pp174-185 London 1986

[27] In my interview with Spinelli in September 1983 the ideas of these three Federal Union activists were cited as having been especially influential.

[28] A. Spinelli *Il Lungo Monologo* in J Pinder *Prophet Not Without Honour: Lothian and the Federal Idea* in The Round Table vol 286 p.217 1983

[29] The Marquis of Lothian *Pacifism is not Enough (nor Patriotism Either)* London 1935 and L Robbins *The Economic Cause of War* London 1939

[30] A Spinelli *The Growth of the European Movement since World War II* in C Grove Haines ed *European Integration* pp36-40 Baltimore 1957

[31] Interview with Spinelli September 1983.

[32] EP Doc A3-47/90

[33] S Mogi *The Problem of Federalism: A Study in the History of Political Theory* pp208-209 London 1931

CHAPTER THREE

Subsidiarity — Essence or Antidote to European Union?

by Anthony Cary

"When it is not necessary to make a law" said Montesquieu, "it is necessary *not* to make a law". The great flood of European legislation released by the Single Market programme — though it is now beginning to dry up — has provoked an understandable reaction. Most people accept that an integrated market requires some regulation at a European level. But they are concerned — and rightly concerned — about the amount of legislation which has been adopted; the level of its detail; the limits of European integration; and the extent to which Community rules are intruding on national life.

The Member States may have chosen, for sound practical reasons, to pool certain powers and decisions. But is all this legislation really necessary, and does it have to be so intrusive?

It is clear that in order to create an entirely level playing field in Europe the Community would have to intervene very extensively. The Commission is besieged by special interest groups, from morticians to insurance salesmen, who demand new regulation to eliminate obstacles to trade in their field. The question we have to ask is whether, in so far as legislation at a European level will introduce Brussels into a further nook and cranny of national life, that is a price worth paying for the expected benefit. This is the crux of the subsidiarity debate. Where do we draw the line? Who draws it? And on what basis? 'Subsidiarity' was described recently in the *Financial Times* as "an unlovely word of uncertain meaning". It has been around a long time, but only entered the public consciousness in 1992.

What is it? Learned articles on its papal origins do not help very much. Article 3b of the Maastricht Treaty is now the *locus classicus*. It is a product of Committee drafting: it has something of the camel about it. And it leaves an awful lot of licence for interpretation in any particular case. It is hardly surprising, then, that people have wanted to translate the principle into practical procedures, checks and balances. The paper on subsidiarity prepared for the Edinburgh Summit attempted to do just that.

Subsidiarity can usefully be described as the 'best level' principle. Before lawmakers set to work, there needs first to be a consensus on the best level for deciding a given policy, and the best level for implementing it. In general, it is

There are at least two fundamental difficulties with subsidiarity as a rule of procedure for applying such principles. First, subsidiarity has been used as a battle-cry by two opposing armies. Crusaders for national sovereignty employ the word as a code for clipping the wings of Brussels, returning power to national parliaments and banishing forever the spectre of European Union.

Crusaders for European federalism, by contrast, see subsidiarity as the very incarnation of the federal principle that powers should be clearly divided between different tiers of Government, some being exercised in the general good at a federal level, and some being reserved, under the constitution, for lower levels of Government, (such as States' rights in the US, or Länder powers in the Federal Republic of Germany).

A further distinction can be drawn, here, between those who would apply the principle of subsidiarity to establish a clear division of responsibilities only between European and national institutions — and those who would go further to apply it to divisions of the power within the Member States, too. That, however, is not the business of the European Community. If Member States, espousing the principle of subsidiarity, choose to stop, arbitrarily, at the national level in its application, that is a matter for them. The Community is conscious of the need to draw on advice and expertise from a sub-national level. That is why a Committee of the Regions is being established by the Maastricht Treaty. Regional identity may be just as powerful a factor in people's sense of identity as loyalty to nation. Ask a Yorkshireman, a Catalonian or a Breton! And the Community can be seen as offering national regions another framework in which to contribute to policymaking, counter-balancing excessive dependence on national capitals. Yet this is not strictly part of the subsidiarity debate in so far as Article 3b of the Maastricht Treaty refers only to the division of responsibilities between the Community and the Member States.

The second conundrum in the debate over subsidiarity is that opinions about the 'best level' for deciding and applying any given policy necessarily reflect political preferences. There is no objectively 'correct' choice about how educational responsibilities should be divided between national, regional or local tiers of government, any more than there is a 'right' choice about whether animal rights, say, should be protected at a national level, a European level, or indeed at a wider international level. One man's level playing field is another man's nook and cranny.

A graphic illustration of this difficulty is provided by Denmark — notoriously Euro-sceptical, and darling of the Bruges Group (if that still exists). The Danes are very keen on subsidiarity. The Edinburgh paper is, in part, a response to their concerns. Yet the Danes want more, not less, environmental policy to be decided at a European level, and more social policy, too. That is an awkward preference, seen from the classic British perspective.

Jeremy Lever QC, when he recently gave evidence to the House of Commons

Foreign Affairs Committee, commented that there is no way we are going to be able to create an algorithm so that you could feed a particular problem over subsidiarity into a very powerful computer and get answers that this should be done at this level, and that at that. Therefore, if there is no objectively correct choice, on what basis should policy makers determine the best level of decision-making in any case?

The federal approach

One response would be to say let us short-circuit the discussion, taking admittedly arbitrary decisions about the best level of decision-making in different areas, but let us then carve our choices in tablets of constitutional stone so that we all know where we stand. That would be the fully federal approach. Although I note that even stone tablets do not end the debate in the USA, where the Tenth Amendment to the Constitution states that anything not explicitly federal shall be up to the States. There is still a ferocious debate about where power should be applied — and the Federal Government still establishes speed limits on State highways, for example.

Yet the European Community is a hybrid system. It combines, that is, elements of the intergovernmentalism and elements of federalism. On the one hand national parliaments are most people's primary democratic focus, and — at least in non-federal states — I am convinced they will remain so for the foreseeable future. On the other hand the nations have chosen to take certain decisions at a European level, to establish a directly-elected European Parliament, and to submit to the authority of the European Court of Justice in Luxembourg.

There is an inherent tension between these two tendencies, which increases in times of recession. The Europhiles and the Europhobes long to resolve the tensions one way or the other. As Sir Leon Brittan put it recently they long to move from the hurly-burly of the Community *chaise longue* to the deep, deep peace whether of twelve separate beds, or of a consummated Union in a very large double one. But there will be no 'resolution' in either sense, for the foreseeable future. And the Community's decision-making system must live with the contradictions. That is why the Community's processes are inevitably complex.

Because the European Community is not a classic federal system, the Commission and the Council have opted not to apply the principle of subsidiarity by drawing up lists of subjects to be dealt with at different levels of Government. Rather, the approach at the Edinburgh Summit is:—

(1)   to settle upon the tests to be applied both to existing and to proposed Community legislation for deciding whether it is appropriate;

(2)   to establish guidelines on how these tests should be applied in the decision-making process;

(3)   to agree procedures and practices to be adopted by the Commission and the Council in this respect.

In addition, the Commission was asked by the European Council meeting in Birmingham in October, to bring forward the first fruits of its examination of existing legislation, or proposals for legislation, where the application of the principle of subsidiarity — as it is now being developed — might argue for amendment, or even repeal.

The tide of European legislation

I have no doubt that we will do well to adopt a dynamic approach of this kind, rather than a static entrenchment of powers for given areas of policy. As in a large company, such choices may, after all, vary with time. At one stage in a company's development it may make sense to carry out certain functions from the centre. At another stage it may be more efficient to set up autonomous profit-centres.

Perhaps it was sensible some years ago to decide, as national ministers unanimously did, that drinking water or bathing-water standards should be established at a European level. It may be, however, that the European level has achieved its purpose, in these cases, of raising standards and public consciousness, and that it would now be less intrusive and less bureaucratic if Member States took back their responsibilities, either completely, or at least by introducing more flexibility in setting the technical parameters, and more national room for manoeuvre in the application of agreed standards.

Leon Brittan — picking up Lord Denning's famous reference to the tide of European legislation — has commented that the legislative mechanisms must allow the tide to go out as well as come in. It would do a great deal to restore public confidence, and to reduce unnecessary fears, if people saw that the process of European integration is not a ratchet enabling Brussels gradually, but inexorably, to extend its power.

I should here clarify a point which is widely misunderstood in Britain and which colours the subsidiarity debate. I spoke just now of people's fear of the inexorable advance of 'Brussels'. For this is the popular perception. Something called 'Brussels' is credited with the glory or the shame for every European development, as if it were a monolithic technocracy (or, in the lurid picture painted in much of the popular press, a Frankenstein, stinking of garlic and bratwurst, which has broken out of the laboratory and is now lurching about the United Kingdom out of democratic control). This picture is nurtured by some national politicians who are all too ready to let Europe take the blame for unpopular policies. That is not necessarily so bad. One of the great advantages of the Community process, indeed, is that it gives national politicians cover for hard decisions (rather as the IMF did for Denis Healey in the mid-1970s). The convergence conditions for Economic and Monetary Union are, for example, already proving helpful to the Italian Government in maintaining pressure to reduce public debt.

Yet the Community is not, in fact, some stern, unbiddable and capricious power. What is popularly called 'Brussels' actually combines two elements: on the one hand, the activities of the European Commission, the European Parliament and other European institutions, including the Court of Justice. And, on the other, the decisions of national elected ministers meeting with their counterparts from other Member States — and the activities of national delegations of civil servants who crawl over every dot and comma of each legislative proposal, and who invariably end up adding dots, commas and codicils of their own to the Commission's original (elegant) ideas. 'Brussels', then, is the shorthand term applied to the structure of cooperation and joint decision-making developed between Member States to pursue their common interests most effectively.

It is important to understand this, because some people are trying to don the armour of subsidiarity in a holy war against the ungodly powers and pretensions of 'Brussels', and of the European Commission in particular. In doing so, they are putting national interests at stake, and regional interests too.

National ministers in the Community process
Almost all the proposals which emerge from the Commission have either been requested by national ministers, meeting in the Council, or fall within the Single Market programme which was laid down by all the heads of government. Only in some 5% or 6% of cases does the Commission bring forward proposals on its own initiative. And once proposals have been tabled, they are, of course, at the mercy of elected ministers, meeting in the Council. The European Parliament has its role to play, but all decisions in the Community rest, ultimately, with national ministers. I am not sure this is understood by the mass of people.

The Commission, conscious of the popular distaste for 'harmonisation' of national systems, which had been the prevailing Community method in the 1970s — and conscious of the difficulty of securing agreement to measures of harmonization — has sought, increasingly, to encourage 'mutual recognition' by Member States of their different national systems. One country may do it this way, and another may do it that way, but that is no obstacle to trade in the Single Market as long as neither seeks to block goods or services from the other because of differences.

The Commission has encouraged this approach wherever possible. Indeed, it may shortly be bringing forward a proposal that all trade between Member States should be automatically accepted on the basis of mutual recognition — along the US pattern — unless a specific health or safety problem could be identified. That is the least intrusive approach that the Community could take, and it is the one that the Commission espouses. But it is the Member States which often have difficulties with it, and insist upon harmonization.

A good recent example concerned motorbikes. Everyone agrees that we need to secure type-approval for motorbikes at a European level, so that they do not need to be made to different specifications for every national market. The industry is crying out for this. Accordingly, the Commission was asked to produce a string of horribly detailed European specifications for everything from motorbike-stands to the placing for number-plates. We went back to the Council to check our orders. Was this really what the nations wanted? Would we not be pilloried in the popular press for this latest Euro-lunacy? Did not subsidiarity apply here? No, we were told, you are to proceed as instructed.

The problem is that each Member State has telephone directories full of detailed national requirements for motorbikes which they are not prepared to relax in the name of mutual recognition. They therefore need European-level regulation of every detail in order to open up the market. But when bikers complain about changes forced upon them, some Ministers will, no doubt, be quick to blame 'Brussels' for this latest assault upon national tradition.

My point here is that the subsidiarity debate is not just about the division of power and responsibility between the nations and the central Community institutions: about Brussels handing things back to the nations. It is, quite as much, about the control exercised by national parliaments over government ministers. At present ministers, like Hilaire Belloc's water-beetle, "glide across the water's face / With ease, celerity and grace", taking some decisions at home and some at a European level, in their wisdom and according to their experience. The national Parliaments want more control over them, and greater clarity about which decisions are taken where. So, indeed, does the European Parliament — from its rather different perspective. All this is about "the power of Brussels" in one sense —but not in the sense generally understood by that phrase, which conjures up pictures of the nations held in thrall by faceless Eurocrats.

The other reason why it is misguided, and even dangerous, for Thatcherite Europhobes to concentrate their venom on the Community institutions — and especially on the European Commission — is that, contrary to popular mythology, the Commission is the champion of open trade within the Community. It is significant, for example, that some of the most vociferous campaigners for a No vote in the French Maastricht referendum were those — like M. Calvet of Peugeot — who are anxious to restore France's ability to protect its national market, and to regain a free hand in subsidising its national companies. Such critics complain of the ultraliberal fanatics in the European Commission, and they long to restore a bit of good old-fashioned market management and central planning.

The Single Market will not yield its expected benefits if it cannot be effectively policed. It needs a strong central authority to see fair play and to stop countries from reintroducing barriers to trade. All Member States —and not least the UK — will be losers if they erode that authority in the name of subsidiarity just as the Single Market is taking shape.

Without burdening the point, I might give two examples. One is in the area of state aids. The Commission has been very much more active, in recent years, in trying to stop Member States from giving certain national companies — national champions, if you will — an unfair advantage over their competitors elsewhere in the Community. This has not been easy. Decisions in this area are often controversial, and will remain so.

Indeed the pressures of the recession, combined with such factors as the temptation for the Federal German Government to pump aid into its new Eastern Länder (say to retain shipbuilding jobs and to expand capacity) are likely to make the job even more controversial. Yet if the Commission does not undertake this job, no-one else will. Member States cannot effectively police their own behaviour, where it may have a national logic, but disadvantages the Community as a whole.

Another example is in the field of liberalization of national monopolies. The Commission has powers, under Article 90 of the Treaty of Rome, to challenge national monopolies in so far as the public good which they are designed to achieve could be attained in ways which would be less destructive of competition. This Article has been used in recent years, for example, to break the stranglehold of some national PTTs over the terminal equipment which can be attached to communications networks, or over the services which can be offered on those networks. Transport and energy too, might benefit from liberalization of this kind, and there is much further to go on telecommunications. Yet a British Telecom spokesman commented the other day that while "the Commission is the main proponent of change in the Community" recent developments — and notably the subsidiarity debate — could blunt its ability to open up the full potential of the Single Market.

The Edinburgh Summit
Let me summarize, finally, some of the ideas developed in the paper on subsidiarity at Edinburgh. The heads of government began by elaborating on the three elements contained in Article 3b of the Maastricht Treaty. First, is a proposed action within the Community's Treaty powers?

Second, if so, should the Community act? The paper suggests a number of tests to be met to justify Community action rather than action at a lower level. The Council, for example, must be satisfied that action at a Community level would produce clear benefits by reason of its scale or effects compared with action at the level of the Member States. In other words, is there added value in taking this action at the level of the Member States? It is not just the question of whether the Treaty allows it, but would there be real value added in doing so?

And third, what should be the nature and extent of the Community action? The paper notes, for example, that financial and administrative burdens should be proportionate to the objective; that Community measures should leave as much scope for national decision as possible; that the form of the action should be as light as possible consistent with the goal; and that where appropriate preferences should be given to cooperation between Member States, and support for such cooperation, rather than centrally coordinated or constraining action.

Sir Leon Brittan, talking recently about the application of subsidiarity in competition policy, said he would like to see more application of EC law by national courts. At the moment, the Commission's DG IV is tremendously burdened by the number of complaints coming to Brussels for rulings. It would really make sense for it to concentrate on cases which by reason of the particular point raised add something to the corpus of European law. We would like to be able to refer to national courts many cases now dealt with at EC level. In due course, national courts might be given the ability to themselves grant exemptions under the competition rules of Article 85.

The Edinburgh paper also examines procedures. The Commission, for example, has for some months now systematically justified its proposals with regard to the principle of subsidiarity. It has also indicated that it will consult more widely before proposing new legislation. It will use more consultation papers (known as green papers), which will ask views on the subsidiarity issue, amongst others, when it consults interested parties.

The Commission may be urged to produce an annual report on the application of subsidiarity. With regard to the Council of Ministers, the Edinburgh Summit asserted that consistency with the principle of subsidiarity should become an integral part of the overall examination of any Commission proposal. Working Group and COREPER reports on a given proposal will, where appropriate, describe how Article 3b has been applied. The European Parliament will be kept fully informed. Finally, there may be a proposal for an Inter-Institutional Agreement between the Commission, the Council and the Parliament to give formal status to such ideas.

These are rather dry procedural matters. The real point is that all those involved in Community work will, I have no doubt, concentrate very much more carefully in future on whether proposals are appropriate; what is the right level for action; and how the objectives might be achieved more simply, with the greatest flexibility, and with the least interference in existing procedures.

In addition, and this is an aspect which could have a more resounding public impact, the Commission presented to the Edinburgh Summit its first ideas on current proposals, and even existing legislation, which might be revised or repealed to reflect the principle of subsidiarity as it is now being developed. The Commission has been asked by heads of government to conduct a full study in this sense by the end of 1993. But the Commission has been asked to come forward at once with its first thoughts.

I do not imagine for a moment that all this is going to banish argument about the limits of Community action. The fundamental differences of view in Europe about what the Community is, and what it should become, are too great for that. Indeed the development of the subsidiarity principle could provoke argument (as the Federal Trust demonstrates) about the limits of national power and the appropriateness of existing national procedures for delegating powers within its own territory.

Nevertheless I am convinced that the debate over subsidiarity will have real, and beneficial, consequences. I do not agree with those who say that subsidiarity is just logic chopping and wording in a Treaty that is going to have no practical impact. There may have been a sense, in the past, in which the European institutions, fighting to develop the Community in the face of entrenched national powers, began to believe that anything which was permitted by the Treaty of Rome must — almost by definition — be to the general good. The Court of Justice encouraged them in that tendency by its maximalist interpretations of the developing Community powers.

As the EC institutions come of age they must recognise that the arguments for action, the reasons for the choice of any particular action, and the proportionality between means and ends, must all be fully developed in every case. The Community should be the stronger for that.

CHAPTER FOUR

Legal Aspects of Subsidiarity in the United Kingdom

by Alan Trench

This chapter will consider some of the legal aspects of implementing the principle of subsidiarity in the United Kingdom by means of some sort of devolved or decentralised government.

The background to the legal problems that arise is the constitutional structure of the UK. The UK is a unitary state, administered by a single government accountable to a single Parliament at Westminster. Many of these administrative acts are carried out without Parliamentary authority, under the Royal prerogative. While some administrative tasks are not carried out by central government but are transferred to lower levels of government which are locally accountable as well, their powers derive from ones Parliament has granted them and this does not reduce the overall importance of Parliament in the constitution.

At the same time, however, three separate legal jurisdictions exist within the UK's territory, each with its own distinct legal system. While Northern Ireland is a common-law jurisdiction, like England and Wales, Scotland is not and has its own quite separate legal tradition and system, and the only point at which all three systems converge is in their use of the House of Lords sitting judicially as the UK's highest civil court. This situation is rather unusual, as most states which have multiple territorial jurisdictions within their territory, such as the United States, have this as a result of a federal structure. The UK does not have this and most constitutional writers are adamant that because of the sovereignty of Parliament this is impossible within the constitution as it is presently exists.

The European Community and Devolution
External pressures are of great importance in pressing the UK to adopt some form of devolved government, especially if this were to lead to some federal or quasi-federal structure. It is therefore necessary to consider how the EC approaches the question of devolved powers within Member States. Regional tiers of government, as well as local government, are to be found in some form in all the larger Member States save the UK, and Community law has to take account of the many different systems of regional government to be found in the Member States. However, the EC has a two-faced attitude toward regional devolution.

It has long since been established that the Community has a separate legal order imposed on the Member States and the Community is not concerned with how those Member States organise themselves internally. Where Member States internally have devolved their powers to lower levels which are autonomous in the exercise of those powers, this has a strange results. In 1991, Belgium was found liable for a breach of its Community obligations because the Walloon region had failed to transpose directives concerning drinking water. The European Court of Justice (ECJ) disregarded the fact that this was an area in which legislative power had been transferred to the provincial communities under the new quasifederal constitution and so the Belgian state could no longer do anything about the problem. From the EC's point of view, Belgium's internal arrangements could not be permitted to interfere with the state's duty to implement its Community obligations.

This point is reinforced by a case concerning subsidised land sold by Derbyshire County Council to Toyota to persuade the company to build its car plant near Derby. This was found by the Commission to constitute an unlawful state aid contrary to Article 92 of the Treaty of Rome and the UK (that is, central government) was required to reclaim this aid from Toyota, even though it had played no part in the original decision to grant the aid. Similar cases have arisen involving other Member States.

It is hard, however, to reconcile this attitude toward devolved government with that embodied in the Maastricht Treaty on European Union, and particularly the Article 3b it inserts into the EEC Treaty. This new article requires that the EC take account of the principle of subsidiarity and that it should not act where decisions should be taken at a lower level. What this clause means is not clear, especially as the principle of subsidiarity is not defined in Article 3b or anywhere else in the Treaty. The UK government, in particular, believes that it is legally enforceable but that it only concerns relations between the Community and the Member States. What effect the clause has will depend on how the ECJ interprets the phrase "the principle of subsidiarity" in its second sentence. If it determines that this phrase adds something to the meaning of the clause, rather than duplicating the procedural definition in the next sub-clause ("only if and insofar as the objectives ..."), the question arises of what it adds. In such a case the meaning of subsidiarity in its substantive sense is at issue. This would, it appears, impose a positive obligation on the Member States to ensure that decisions were taken at the lowest appropriate level. If a Member State did not have a body at the appropriate level, it would have to establish one, with the necessary powers and resources to discharge the tasks with which it was charged, or face being in breach of its Community obligations. The Maastricht Treaty also alters Article 171 of the Treaty of Rome to enable the ECJ to fine Member States which are in default of their Community obligations.

Devolution and the Structure of the UK
The UK's structure would govern how any system of devolved or decentralised power would work, whether this were introduced because of domestic political pressures or because of external legal or political ones.

England for legal purposes is and always has been a unitary state. Wales became legally fully part of England by 1536, following annexation in 1284, and while it enjoys administrative devolution and some special treatment at Westminster, there is no substantive legal difference between England and Wales.

Devolution to the English regions or to Wales would face the same problems, which stem from the application of the doctrine of the sovereignty of Parliament as understood by lawyers, most of whom still subscribe to Dicey's account in *The Law of the Constitution* and who give little support to challenges to it. The doctrine means that there is nothing that Parliament properly constituted cannot do, save to bind future Parliaments. Parliament's power extends to altering the constitution of the UK, which consists of an accretion of Acts of Parliament along with unwritten sources such as constitutional conventions. As a result, Parliament may simply establish any system of decentralised power that it wishes, and bodies can be created by Act of Parliament to exercise whatever powers and functions Parliament transfers to them. The powers such a body exercises can be very broad in scope and will not be subject to challenge unless there is some defect in the original legislation, or the body exceeds the powers which are transferred to it, or it does not exercise the powers in accordance with the legislation.

The rules governing this are well known as they are the basis of administrative law in the UK, and are similar whether they apply to a Minister's use of statutory powers or the exercise of them by a local authority. In essence, these provide that a statutory corporation such as a local authority may commit acts which are not expressly authorised in the Act of Parliament creating it, provided that they are incidental to the authorised acts or to the functions which it exercises. If they are not, the acts will be ultra vires and unlawful. These limits are applied fairly narrowly by the courts, however. However, a Northern Irish case suggests that in the case of a "subordinate legislature" the ultra vires rules are considerably relaxed. Here, the House of Lords held that when the substance of an Act of a subordinate legislature was within the powers granted to it, the Act would not be invalidated "merely because incidentally it affects matters which are outside the authorized field". The powers delegated to Stormont under the Government of Ireland Act 1920 were extensive ones in any event. However, "subordinate legislature" is not defined either in the judgement in this case or in the Government of Ireland Act, so it is unclear whether it would include bodies like the regional assemblies for England or Wales.

There is no reason why the powers transferred to a number of different lower-level authorities must be the same in each case, as was shown by the different powers given to Scotland and Wales in the Scotland Act 1978 and the Wales Act 1978, so there is no legal objection to variable powers being transferred, as is the case with the Spanish autonomous communities.

However, the powers conferred by Act of Parliament can be taken away just as easily, as no Parliament can fetter future Parliaments. Therefore, if subsidiarity were implemented by means of Acts of Parliament which simply created new bodies to exercise certain powers given to it by statute, there could be no way of ensuring that the procedures for the exercise of powers transferred would not be changed, that the powers themselves would remain the same, nor that the conditions and financial arrangements under which they were exercised would continue. Attempts to draft legislation in such a way as to prevent its repeal save by onerous procedures would not succeed; in 1934 the Court of Appeal held that, where Parliament in an Act purported to provide that inconsistent provisions of later legislation should not be applied, the earlier Act was impliedly repealed by a later inconsistent Act. Ministers' use of the Crown prerogative or of their statutory powers might add to confusion about the extent and application of an assembly's powers. As a consequence, any sort of decentralisation of power to Wales or the regions of England (or to a subordinate Scottish assembly) would be at the continued discretion of Parliament, or rather at that of the government of the day commanding a majority in the House of Commons. The experience of local government in the 1980s demonstrates how even a well-established relationship of this nature can be profoundly altered by Ministerial action with or without Acts of Parliament. Devolution of power to the regions of the UK will not be meaningful if it is vulnerable to alteration almost on a whim in this way.

Further, the subordinate legislatures' exercise of the powers granted to them would remain firmly subject to those of Westminster. The devolved assemblies could not lawfully seek to change the rules governing their operation without Parliament's consent. In 1932 an attempt by a newly-elected Australian state government to alter an Act of the New South Wales legislature, which had established a procedure for the repeal of a specific provision, and with which the repealing Act did not comply, failed as the Colonial Laws Validity Act 1865 required that the repeal be "in the manner and form laid down by a colonial or imperial legislation in force at the time". A 1952 South African case considered the implied repeal by a later South African Act of entrenched provisions of the South Africa Act 1909, enacted at Westminster. The South African Appellate Division held that those provisions could only be repealed by following the procedure laid down in the Westminster Act of Parliament. These decisions mean that the autonomy of regional assemblies would exist only within limits prescribed by Parliament, which the regional assembly could not change. Parliament could, however, be change them at any time and so the assemblies would always depend on the goodwill of Parliament.

The situation would be different if the devolution of power led to a fundamental transformation in the political and legal structure of the UK. As Sir William Wade points out, the questions of whether an Act can be repealed is dependent on legal reality; if political circumstances transform the meaning of a piece of legislation, it will not be capable of being repealed because the courts would not accept that the repeal was valid. The Statute of Westminster 1931 is most often cited in this context; as it freed the Dominions from legislation by the Westminster Parliament, it cannot be revoked save by their consent. Even if Parliament purported to repeal it, the gesture would be meaningless.

The transfer of authority to regions would also greatly affect the operation of the Royal prerogative. If the transfer arose because of domestic factors, it would be subject to interference by central government in executive acts because of the prerogative. If it were because of external circumstances, such as the application of the new Article 3b of the Treaty of Rome discussed above, the transfer would have to take precedence over the exercise of the Royal prerogative, with consequences which would be far-reaching but impossible to foresee in any detail.

Northern Ireland is a separate jurisdiction from England and Wales but also a common-law one. It has experience of life under a separate Parliament operating under statutory powers, from 1920 to the resumption of direct rule from London in 1972. This experiment was not successful politically or constitutionally, but this failure is attributable more to the particular circumstances of the province than to any inherent legal or political flaws of devolution, although the system adopted meant that the weaknesses of devolved power were exaggerated.

It is interesting to note how the powers of the Northern Irish government as defined in statute were treated. McCrudden notes that a constitutional convention developed that Westminster did not concern itself with powers devolved to Northern Ireland, although these powers were shared and the Acts in question, the Government of Ireland Act 1920 and the Northern Ireland Act 1949, were carefully drafted not to exclude Westminster's intervention in these areas. Whether this might be followed in other cases of devolution by statute is unlikely, as this is probably due to Northern Ireland's particular circumstances rather than any other factor. In any case, whether such a convention would be binding or could be enforced is highly doubtful.

Scotland's links with England began with a personal union of the crowns under James I of England and VI of Scotland in 1603, formalised in the Act of Union of 1707. The Act of Union provides expressly for Scotland's rights and identity to continue even though the power to legislate was transferred to Westminster, and although public law was to be the same throughout the United Kingdom, Scots private law was to remain unaltered by the Union except when it was necessary "for the evident utility of the subjects in Scotland". The distinction between public and private law rights is a complex one. The highest Scots court, the Court of Session, has held that in principle questions arising under the Act of Union are in general justiciable by the Court of Session. However, when Article XVIII of the Act of Union was considered by the lower Outer House of the Court of Session in 1975, the issue of whether a particular Act contravened the Act of Union was held not to be justiciable. (This is counter to the argument that the Act of Union defines the terms of the union of Scotland and England and that Acts of Parliament therefore can be ultra vires the Act of Union.)

The status of Scotland means that it would be easy to establish a system under which extensive powers would be granted to a Scottish assembly, although the relationship of this assembly with Westminster would be fraught with problems. The powers of such an assembly would be subject to many of the same considerations discussed above in the context of England and Wales. An assembly would not threaten the Act of Union unless it sought to alter public law in Scotland, as the Act of Union provides that this has to be the same throughout the UK. However, its internal powers would be restricted by Article XVIII while the Act of Union remained in force, and Scottish Acts would not bind successors of the Scots parliament.

Nonetheless, if a parliament (even in name only) were established, this could raise difficult problems. Even the partial transfer of sovereignty to Scotland would limit that of Westminster, which is legally unacceptable at present. A parliament with no sovereignty would probably not be acceptable politically or be worthy of the name. Ultimately it would be necessary for the courts to accept that the Westminster Parliament could limit its sovereignty and had done so by establishing such an assembly. There are precedents for this in the way that the Dominions' autonomy was accepted even prior to the Statute of Westminster, without considering whether they had precisely complied with the powers transferred by statute or not.

If Scotland were to be granted independence by Act of Parliament, repealing the Union with Scotland Act 1706, this Act would not be capable of any meaningful repeal in law as well as in fact. However, implementing Scottish independence would require some care and the steps by which this would be achieved would need to be specified in the Act of Parliament. This would need to specify which Scottish institutions would acquire what legal powers on the day of independence. A written constitution would not be needed for this, provided the institutions to which the powers would be transferred already existed and the arrangements could be specified with enough detail to make them work. In reality this would probably mean that a written constitution would be needed, however.

The Act would need careful drafting in other respects, too. It would need to provide for Union legislation extending to Scotland to continue to apply in Scotland, pending Acts of the Scottish Parliament to amend or repeal these laws, while providing that Union legislation would continue to apply in the remnant of the Union (Northern Ireland and England and Wales). It would also need to provide for the continuation in force in Scotland, at least for the time being, of many principles of English law, especially public law, pending their alteration by Scottish institutions. The constitutional status of what was left following Scottish independence should not be altered, however; the United Kingdom would not cease to exist, as the old Scottish and English Kingdoms did in 1707, but would consist henceforth only of Northern Ireland and England and Wales.

It is a general principle of international law that successor states may inherit the treaty commitments of their predecessor. However, the Treaty of Rome does not provide for the direct accession of a successor state of a Member State to the European Communities and there is therefore no existing mechanism to deal with this. The Scottish National Party has obtained legal advice that, as a successor state to the UK, independent Scotland would be able to accede directly to the EC. The situation is not as straightforward as the SNP believes, however. First, accession by this means depends on Scotland being in law a successor to the UK rather than a new state, which cannot be taken for granted. Second, it ignores the fact that membership of the EC is much more complex than membership of other international organisations. The terms of membership, especially the financial ones, are very important in joining the Community, as the UK's experience since accession shows. Providing for suitable terms of membership would require considerable negotiation. A parallel situation has resulted from the division of Czechoslovakia. The newly-established Czech and Slovak Republics decided to renegotiate the Association Agreement the former federal state had concluded with the EC, although they could have treated the old agreement as continuing.

There is no inherent reason why these negotiations should not begin before Scotland became independent, but there would be considerable practical difficulties. The Community would need to know that the terms of accession would be such that the new member could adhere to them practically and would be willing to do so politically. It is questionable whether any 'government in waiting', even a democratically elected one, could satisfy these requirements. The direct implementation of 'independence in Europe' must therefore be regarded as unrealistic.

Devolved Government and the Courts

Any system for implementing subsidiarity will inevitably lead to legal disputes about the extent of the powers of the various levels of government and their relations with each other. It is therefore necessary to consider what courts would consider these questions and how they would approach them. Traditionally in England, issues of public law have been subject to the same rules as private law and considered in the same courts. This has been extended to the whole of the UK, and is quite different to, say, France, where there is a separate system of courts for public-law matters and a separate set of legal rules for them to use. The practical difficulties that result from such an approach have led most (but not all) issues of public law to be subject to special rules of court, separately listed in the Queen's Bench Division of the High Court and handled by a specialist body of judges. Are such arrangements likely to be adequate for systems of the sort which are being considered here?

The framers of the Scotland Act did not think so. This gave the Judicial Committee of the Privy Council jurisdiction to hear appeals in cases about the working of the Acts. All the Lords Justices of Appeal as well as the Lords of Appeal in Ordinary (the Law Lords) are members of the Privy Council and would be eligible to sit on this body. This use of the Privy Council would have been quite novel, as it has usually dealt with appeals from the Commonwealth (particularly in criminal matters) and from professional associations such as the General Medical Council in disciplinary matters. Using it as the highest constitutional court would mean that the body dealing with such questions is not the same as that which deals with questions of administrative law. This could result in legal anomalies, as the ordinary courts might develop one approach and the Privy Council a different one. The prospect of different rules of law being applied in Canada was a reason for the Privy Council holding in 1947 that Canada could end appeals to it from state as well as federal courts in criminal matters.

The powers of the Privy Council derive from the Royal prerogative (strictly, the Privy Council only advises the Crown on what to do in a particular case), and this usually gives it power to reverse its own decisions, but the position will be different when the jurisdiction is conferred by statute. Schedule 12, clause 25, of the Scotland Act provided that "a decision of the Judicial Committee ... shall be binding in all subsequent legal proceedings", which suggests that the doctrine of precedent is more binding for Privy Council decisions in such matters than it is for House of Lords ones, as the Privy Council would not be able to reverse its own previous decisions. The fact that the Privy Council's powers stem from the prerogative may also lead to problems if the existence and operation of the prerogative are called into question by external factors requiring the implementation of subsidiarity.

Legal issues have often been ignored in discussions about decentralising government in Britain. This makes such discussions utopian rather than of practical use. The aim of this chapter has been to highlight some of the graver difficulties that would have to be overcome if any scheme for implementing subsidiarity in Britain is to be realised.
The fact that these difficulties are in some cases very serious should not be taken to mean that they are legally insuperable. Almost any scheme would require alteration of the British constitution to work, but the adaptability of the unwritten constitution is its greatest strength. Ultimately, however, the strength of regional government will depend on how subsidiarity is applied by the EC, and on political changes within the United Kingdom

---

Books and Articles

V Bogdanor *Devolution* Oxford 1979
ECS Wade and AW Bradley *Constitutional and Administrative Law* Longman 1985
AW Bradley *The Sovereignty of Parliament - in Perpetuity?* in J Jowell and D Oliver   eds *The Changing Constitution* Oxford 1989
C Cross and SB Cross *Local Government Law* Sweet & Maxwell 1986
RFV Heuston *Essays in Constitutional Law* Stevens 1964

JP Mackintosh *The Devolution of Power* Penguin 1968

D Marquand *Regional Devolution* in Jowell & Oliver *Changing Constitution*
    pp371-384

C McCrudden *Northern Ireland and the British Constitution* in Jowell & Oliver
    Changing Constitution pp297-42

TB Smith *The Union of 1707 as fundamental law* in Public Law pp99-121 1957

H Street & R Brazier eds *De Smith Constitutional and Administrative Law*
Penguin   1985

AG Toth *The principle of subsidiarity in the Maastricht Treaty* in Common
Market   Law Review vol.29 pp.1079-1105 1992

M Upton *Marriage Vows of the Elephant: the Constitution of 1707* in Law
Quarterly   Review pp79-103 1989

HWR Wade *The Basis of Legal Sovereignty* in Cambridge Law Journal pp172-197
    1955

Scottish National Party *Independence in Europe - Make It Happen Now!* The
    Manifesto of the SNP Edinburgh 1992

Cases

Attorney-General for New South Wales v Trethowan [1932] AC p526

Attorney-General for Ontario v Attorney-General for Canada [1947] 1 All E R
137

Ellen Estates Ltd v Minister of Health [1934] K.B p 590

Gallagher v Lynn [1937] A C p 863

Gibson v Lord Advocate [1975] Scottish Law Times p 134

Harris v Minister of the Interior 1952 (2) S A p 429

MacCormick v Lord Advocate [1953] Scottish Law Times p 255

Case 26/62 Van Gend en Loos [1962] E C R p 1

Statutes

The Union with Scotland Act 1706 6 Anne c 11

The Judicial Committee Acts 1833 3 & 4 Will 4 c 41

The Judicial Committee Acts 184 4 7 & 8 Vict c 69

The Colonial Laws Validity Act 1865 28 & 28 Victoria c 63

The Judicial Committee Act 1881 44 & 45 Vict c 3

The Government of Ireland Act 1920 10 & 11 Geo 5 c 67

The Scotland Act 1978 1978 c 51

The Wales Act 1978 1978 c 52

CHAPTER FIVE

Europe of the Regions

Subsidiarity in Belgium
by Annemie Neyts-Uyttebroeck MP

I have been invited by the Federal Trust to offer some views on the ongoing process of institutional reform in Belgium and to outline for you whether and how this process relates to the concept of subsidiarity. I shall address the subsidiarity issue both in its national or interior aspect, as well as in its European or exterior aspect. I shall consider subsidiarity in relation between European, national, regional and local authorities. I will try to highlight some of the intricacies of the institutional evolution in Belgium, and will in the course of that offer some dissonant, if not disturbing views.

Let me first limit myself to the internal institutional evolution of my small, but nevertheless complicated home country Belgium. Belgium is indeed a 'surprise package', to quote a CNN advertisement, which however refers not to our institutional surprises, but to the charms of my country as a holiday destination. So let us concentrate on Belgium as it was allowed to emerge from the London Conference in 1830-1831.

Belgium came into existence in 1830, after a short and not too violent revolution which threw out the Dutch from our country — with whom we had been joined in 1815 by the Vienna Conference after the defeat of Napoleon at Waterloo. Some of the Belgian revolutionaries had dreamt of joining France; others preferred independence; but it was indeed the London Conference which decided that an independent Belgium would be a convenient buffer to contend the mighty French. And so Belgium declared itself independent and the Founding Fathers, assembled in a national Conference, set out to write a Constitution.

The Belgian Constitution of 1831 organised three levels of authority, the local or municipal level, the provincial level and the national level. At each level there was an elected council or parliament, and an executive or government. Tradition has it that Nineteenth Century Belgium was a nation of the highly centralised, French-inspired Jacobin type.

Be that as it may, our Constitution said that local authorities, our communes, regulate "all matters of local concern", and that the provincial authorities would and could regulate "all matters of provincial concern". Nothing being said very precisely about the national authorities, it was presumed that they could regulate all the rest. To complete the picture, I must add that the three level system was organised as a pyramid, the provincial authorities controlled the communal authorities while they themselves were controlled by the national government.

This way of distinguishing levels and areas of competence between different authorities constituted probably a very practical and pragmatic approach to what we have come to call 'subsidiarity' — to the local authorities, matters of local concern, to the provincial authorities, matters of provincial concern, with nothing precisely being said about the national level which, however, is in charge of the legislation. Under this system, the local and provincial authorities have enjoyed a large measure of autonomy so long as our national government counted no more than five to six or seven members. There just were not enough ministers to meddle in most local or provincial affairs. And there were no telephones, nor cars, just some trains — and this proved very beneficial to subsidiarity too.

As with all idyllic and probably idealised situations, this one did not last long. One reason was that the newly established Belgian state completely disregarded the fact that Belgium was a nation of two languages, two cultures and possibly two peoples.

The 1831 Belgian Constitution gave the status of official language only to French, in complete disregard of the fact that a majority of Belgians, those living in the Northern part of the country and in Brussels, spoke Flemish. The Flemish struggle for recognition of its language and culture started to gain momentum in the last quarter of the Nineteenth Century. From then on, the institutional debate in Belgium no longer concentrated on the repartition and devolution of power between the three traditional levels of power — local, provincial and national. The whole institutional debate and the ensuing institutional reforms focused henceforward on the question of how to accommodate the institutional organisation of our country to two, and then three languages and cultures. (It should not indeed be forgotten that after World War I Belgium gained a small territory of formerly German communes.)

Belgium first tried to accommodate the linguistic aspirations of the Belgians by using their own languages, Flemish or French or German, in administrative and education-matters. The first comprehensive linguistic laws date back to 1932. They established four linguistic regions: the unilingual Flemish, French and German regions, and the bilingual linguistic region of Brussels. These laws were further developed and refined in 1962, 1963, 1966 and 1988. It appeared quickly however that the aspirations of the Flemish, Walloon and Brussels' Belgians went further than the desire to use their own language in matters of education, culture and administration. They wanted more political autonomy to define their own cultural and economic policies. These aspirations have fuelled the process of institutional reform which has been marked by structural constitutional changes in 1970-71, 1980, 1988 — and now 1993.

It is important to recall that all Belgian political parties split along linguistic lines at the end of the 1960s and early 70s. Today we have two liberal parties, two socialist parties, two Christian Democrat parties, two green or ecologist parties. We do have, moreover, two distinct public opinions, a Flemish-speaking one and a French-speaking one and I am sorry to say that they know little about each other.

Besides having linguistic regions, Belgium has three political regions — the so-called communities — which do not overlap each other. Moreover, the institutional organisation of Flemish-speaking Belgium is different from that of French-speaking Belgium.

In Flemish-speaking Belgium, there is a single council and executive, competent in regional, cultural, and education matters. In French-speaking Belgium, there are, as distinct bodies, a community council and executive, competent for cultural and education matters — plus a Walloon regional council and executive, competent for regional (that is mainly economic and environmental) matters. In the German linguistic region (where some 60,000 German-speaking Belgians live) there is a German community council and executive competent for cultural and education matters. Finally, the region of the capital city of Brussels has a regional council and executive which are competent both for regional matters and for common cultural and welfare matters.

All these legislative and executive bodies exercise powers which formerly belonged to the national legislature and executive. There is, moreover, no hierarchy between, for instance, a French or Flemish cultural or economic decree, a Brussels economic ordinance and a national law. The respective limitations are territorial or sectoral, not hierarchical. This means that the Belgian federal system does not, unlike the German one, recognise the principle that "Bundesrecht bricht Landesrecht".

Conflicts of competence are decided upon by the newly established Arbitration Court which will in due time evolve into a Constitutional Court. Conflicts of interest are not submitted to a specific jurisdiction but are settled by coordination and cooperation between regions, communities and the federal state. Those conflicts which have occurred have invariably been settled through political negotiations between parties rather than through institutional procedures. Invariably too, these political negotiations have resulted in expensive compromises.

So, what exactly is going on in Belgium? Belgium is actually going through a slow and painstaking process of federalisation. Belgium is transforming itself from a hierarchically organised and centralised nation into a form of federalism without any hierarchy — that is to say, the federated components are on one and the same level of authority and power as the federal state. In the absence of any hierarchy, conflicts of competence are settled by the Court of Arbitration while conflicts of interests are settled by political negotiation.

Moreover, the old, three level system of government — national, provincial and local — has subsisted alongside this federalization. But the federated components — the regions and communities — are increasingly replacing the old Brussels-based national state. So the Flemish, Walloon and Brussels communes and provinces are now controlled by the Flemish, Walloon and Brussels' executives. The provinces are being side-lined, to the extent that Brussels may well withdraw from Brabant. Needless to say, the present institutional organisation of Belgium has become extremely complicated and difficult to understand.

How does this process relate to subsidiarity or to put it more bluntly, what has this process done to subsidiarity? Firstly, the relationship between the national, and regional/community level. Here, the redistribution of competences and financial means has gone from the national authorities to the regional/community authorities. As all these authorities operate on the same level (the only difference being a difference of territorial scale), the transfer of power and resources has been more lateral than downwards. As a consequence, power has come no nearer to the public.

From the point of view of the individual citizen, one must conclude that the political and administrative decision-making process has remained just as distant as before. However, from the point of view of collective or community interests, it is undeniable that the federal organisation of Belgium has made it possible to accommodate their differing views on economic, welfare, education, cultural policy, and so on.

If the accommodation of diversity should be one of the main aims and virtues of subsidiarity, in that sense the Belgian reforms are succeeding. If we consider that subsidiarity should bring the decision-making process nearer to those affected by the decisions, I am much less optimistic. It is for instance characteristic that the Belgian local authorities have never been so tightly controlled as they now are by their 'own' executives. Their autonomy has never been so reduced as it is nowadays. It is no exaggeration to say that the Flemish, Walloon and Brussels' executives practice a heavy centralisation, which is entirely of their own making.

How does the Belgian process of institutional reform affect the relationship between party political decision-making and constitutional-institutional evolution? It should come as no surprise that the almost permanent institutional debate and the ensuing reforms of the Constitution and of institutional legislation have, if anything, greatly increased the weight of party political decision-making.

I have said in a parliamentary debate that we now live in a situation where the political negotiations and political compromises come first, and where the Constitution and institutional legislation not only come second, but where they are adapted and changed (I said "twisted") to accommodate the political compromises. This has damaged the status of the Constitution and of the institutional legislation. They have become mere texts which a political coalition can change at will, if it so decides. The Belgian Constitution has ceased to be an almost intangible text which was kept at a safe distance from party political negotiating. I am not sure that this is a happy state of affairs.

Finally, I want to offer some views on the effects all this seems to have on the electorate. One might reflect that Belgian institutional organisation is now almost as complicated as that which the Treaties of Rome and Maastricht have put into place for the European Community. This would be for similar reasons: it is no easy thing to keep together three regions, three languages, cultures and peoples within the framework of one single country. It is of course much more difficult to bring together twelve different states and nine different languages.

It is moreover no easy thing to convince any given authority — be it local council, regional body or national government and parliament — to give up the tiniest bit of power and the smallest amount of money or competence. And when different views, taboos, prejudices, ideals, not to forget emotions are represented around the negotiating table, one is bound to end up with an intricate and complicated construction. What most political negotiations generally forget in the course of their labours, is that they are being watched and coolly judged — not only by their own parties and parliamentary groups, but by the general public. If they resort to arcane circumlocutions in order not to displease their parties, the public will not comprehend — and finally reject — the outcome.

For Belgium, it is its survival as a nation which is at stake. For the European Community, the real issue is its economic and political role in the world. Both need to clarify their real issues and challenges. Both need to explain better that change is inevitable if we are to survive. Both need to pay much more attention to the quality of the institutions we create. Subsidiarity may be a tool to enhance the quality of our institutions and of their interaction.

I hope that this testimony from a small country which is federalising itself in order to survive has not discouraged those of you who advocate institutional reforms in Britain. Be assured that I had no such intention.

The Application of Subsidiarity
by Carles Alfred Gasòliba i Böhm MEP

European public opinion has displayed growing reservations in the face of the possibility that the road to European Union may lead to a model which is centralized, imposes uniformity, is inefficient and places increasing importance on the new Brussels-based bureaucracy.

This perception has been put to great use by opponents of the ratification of the

Maastricht Treaty, who have rightly based their theses on some of the decisions of the European Community which demonstrate an excess of the interventionist spirit. Although it is very difficult to find a suitable balance between the creation of European unity and total respect for the powers and responsibilities attributed to the existing administrations, everyone agrees that new, excessive European bureaucracy is to be avoided. The European Parliament, aware of this underlying problem, came to grips with it by approving Giscard d'Estaing's report on the application of the principle of subsidiarity in 1991. Fortunately, this initiative was incorporated by the Council of Ministers into the Treaty, defining subsidiarity in Article 3b.

Like any constitutional principle, the definition of subsidiarity is very broad and depends on the contemporary political forces present in the Community. This is why attempts to define the content and application of the principle have led to different positions being taken up by some governments, such as, firstly, the British position, which in fact implies a devolution of the powers and responsibilities of the Commission to the states. Secondly, there is the position which supports the application of the principle, but limits it to relations between the Community and the states. And thirdly, the position which sees the extension of the principle to the regions.

Undoubtedly, therefore, subsidiarity is one of the key notions in understanding the scope and meaning of the Treaty of Maastricht. In the course of the Intergovernmental Conferences, discussion centred around the definition of the notion of subsidiarity as a guideline for more democratic guarantees in the process of European construction, and in its two-fold role of criterion for political action and principle for the generation of legal obligations.

In fact, one of the most important questions considered was the need for the Treaty to try to respond to the general fear, shared by some member governments and their public opinions, that the process of moving towards European unity may imply an excessive centralisation towards Community administration. There was the impression that the EC was trying unjustifiably to bring into line aspects which were very deeply rooted in the singular nature of each state. The Treaty of Maastricht, by especially incorporating the principle of subsidiarity into the basic legal texts for the first time, has provided a positive answer to these problems. It presents specific criteria of political and legal evaluation as to what the limits on future powers and responsibilities of the Community should be within the dynamics of European integration.

The aim of the introduction of subsidiarity into the Treaty has been to place a limit on the non-democratic extension of the future powers and responsibilities of the Community. This took place precisely at the time that a new phase was being undertaken on the path to European unity, characterized by deeper integration among Member States, above all in economic and monetary aspects. The limit on the expansion of EC powers and responsibilities does not arise from a strict political decision to impede this expansion in itself, but from a concern that the entire process of Community construction be carried out with a guarantee of effectiveness and democratic legitimacy; that is to say, that decisions will be made by levels of political representation and legitimacy — at Community or state level — which are more suited to achieving the hoped-for results.

Nonetheless, different question marks hang over the practical application of the principle of subsidiarity. Whose job will it be to decide whether an action is more effective if carried out by the Community or by the separate Member States? Who will be responsible for ensuring control of this principle? And what will be the practical consequences of its application?

The adoption of Community decisions always involves a process of permanent negotiation among its various institutions. The introduction of subsidiarity will simply mean that each new legislative act of the Community will be examined and that the Commission and the Council will have to respect it both in word, as a legal restriction, and in spirit, as a political assessment. Furthermore, precisely because of its legally binding nature, the interpretation of this principle and its application to individual cases will be guaranteed by the intervention of the Court of Justice, which will exercise a major role in specifying the content, limits and practical working of the principle.

Finally, the logic behind the notion of subsidiarity could encourage the decentralisation of decision-making processes between the Community and the European regions, because the desire for effectiveness in political management and respect for diversity in the European construction have their counterpart in regional entities as differentiated territorial areas, in many cases entirely suitable for the application of Community policies. However, this possibility depends essentially on the political determination of member governments.

Different states, among them Germany and the United Kingdom, insisted on the introduction of this principle during negotiation of the Treaty of Maastricht. The UK hoped to slow down the process of EC integration and even reduce its scope. (Major spoke of "scrapping" part of Community legislation in force.) It was even said, in British quarters, that subsidiarity would help to overcome Denmark's mistrust of Maastricht, though Denmark itself had never used these arguments, nor had it shown itself to be particularly interested in the principle. Germany, on the other hand, defended the role of the regions in drawing up and applying Community law when the powers and responsibilities of the Länder were affected and insisted on the importance of the sub-state and regional levels. Spain takes a very rigid position, and considers that subsidiarity should not be applied internally or affect the division of powers and responsibilities between the Spanish state and Spanish Autonomous Communities or regions.

The European Parliament considers that the notion of subsidiarity must not be applied to renationalize Community politics. It also believes that neither the EC's scope nor institutional balance should be questioned. As regards the regions, the Commission wants an important role for the future Committee of the Regions. The European regions, which are taking on a growing political role in the Community as a whole, have increasingly defended both their institutional recognition within the Community itself and their desire to take part actively in the process of European construction.

Since the creation of the European Community in the 1950s, a slow but sure process of political and administrative decentralisation has been taking place in several Member States in favour of Länder, nations, autonomous communities and regions with the power to make laws. These regions, like Catalonia, are directly affected by European integration in that they participate directly in EC Councils of Ministers. The regions have demonstrated their concern at the possibility of being left out of the EC process. In response to this situation, the Treaty of Maastricht created the Regions Committee which, despite its initial limitations, will allow the organisation of opinions and the channelling of interests of the regions. The regions will therefore, for the first time, have an advisory body to represent them at Community level, which will have to be consulted in many matters.

This has been possible thanks to the position adopted by certain European states, such as Germany and Belgium. But also worthy of mention is the work of the Assembly of European Regions, whose president is currently Mr Jordi Pujol, President of the Generalitat, the Government of Catalonia, who, since the Assembly was founded in 1985, has promoted the role of European Regions in the creation of European Union.

The Assembly of European Regions, aware of the changes being wrought in Europe, as well as defending the need to promote European Union, has emphasised the fact that it should be based on a federal model with a well-balanced structure which takes into consideration the three levels: federal union, Member States and nations and regions. It recommends: (1) a division of powers and responsibilities clearly laid-out according to the principle of subsidiarity; (2) the right of the regions to initiate and cooperate in the European decision-making process to the extent that their rights and interests are affected; (3) the creation of regional electoral constituencies; and (4) the defence and guarantee of regional language and cultural rights.

There are strong arguments in favour of institutionalizing the regional level in the design of the new Community. The very existence of the regional dynamic in western Europe is evidence of the crisis and insufficiency of the state as a model of political organization. The force of the regional phenomenon arises from a social and individual need for self-identity. In addition, the changes brought about in Central and Eastern Europe will strengthen political decentralisation even further, because they are mainly loosely joined, plurinational entities which have recognised, in the state, an instrument which centralizes and monopolises all social initiatives.

The creation of the Single Market could increase regional North-South and East-West disparities. In this context, the regional level becomes a geographical and institutional area which is more suited to drawing up and applying regional policy to promote both growth and economic and social cohesion. For this reason, the strengthening of EC powers and responsibilities should be accompanied by the participation of regional authorities in the adoption of decisions which affect them. Better information and increased citizen participation in EC policies would increase the respect for the powers and responsibilities granted to the regions by their respective state Statutes of Autonomy. Moreover, regional participation in the process of drawing up Community regulations is the best guarantee for the correct application of EC law in the regions. Lastly, vital for the existence of European cultural citizenry and identity is the respect for diversity of cultures and languages present within Europe, where various examples of plurinational states can be found.

The Generalitat of Catalonia established the Patronat Català Pro Europa in 1982 with the aim of training, informing and making Catalan society aware of the European Community. The Patronat, of which I am secretary-general, is made up of senior representatives of the Catalan government, local authorities, business and academia. Spain's joining the EC in 1986 led the Patronat to progress from providing general information to taking thorough control of EC initiatives that affect Catalonia, with all the implications and requirements of membership. To carry out its various duties the Patronat has developed a close working relationship with the Community's institutions, and has set up a Brussels delegation. It has also decentralized its own services within Catalonia.

From a Catalan point of view, like the Germans, it would be very useful for us to have a kind of trip-wire for the application of not only Spanish but also EC rules. We already have exclusive competence in education, health care, environment, urban planning, public works, infrastructure construction and so on. If we can preserve our competences allowed by the new Spanish constitution of 1980, we must try to avoid the clawing back of powers by central EC government.

Nonetheless, greater regional participation does not mean that the states would lose their place. It is simply a question of considering a new conception of the state in a structure which also takes into account the regional level. This is a complex, highly political matter which depends essentially on the political determination of the Member States to open the way up to the greater involvement of the peoples and citizens of Europe. The Treaty of Maastricht, with its principle of subsidiarity, is the key to the opening up of the Community to popular participation — and to increasing levels of public support.

The German Federal Experience
by Otto Schmuck

I have recently taken up a new position in the Ministry for European and Domestic Affairs of one of the Länder, Rheinland Pfalz. All the German Länder now have ministries dealing with European affairs, and there is a new regular conference bringing these ministers together. On 2 December 1992 we had our debate on the Maastricht agreement in the Bundestag, in which, as in all important debates, not only national parliamentarians but also ministers from the Länder are allowed to speak. In the Bundestag hemicircle, there is the President as usual in the middle, with national ministers on the one side, and, on the other, in the same quality seats, the representatives of the Länder. On 2 December the Bundestag ratified the Treaty, but we had a second debate in the Bundesrat, which represents the Länder, on 18 December. If the Länder said no, the Treaty would not be ratified.

In the Maastricht debate, we had a majority in the Bundestag of 95% — with only some of the PDS, the former Communists in the new five Länders and some of the Greens against. European integration was the way the Germans after the Second World War had the possibility of coming back into the family of countries. And it was clear for the Germans that German unification was only possible within the European framework. We needed to demonstrate to the outside world that we were an independent but not an irresponsible nation.

Although everyone is in favour of Maastricht, however, there are some fears that we are losing our Deutschmark. The Bundestag and later on the Bundesrat as well will have a new debate at the moment when the third stage of EMU is reached. The government will be asked to adopt the position of both Houses. This means that the Länder will even have a say in the economic field which is not normally one of the competences of the regions. The second point which is very important for Germans is the democratic deficit. Transfers of competences to the European level means that the European Parliament should become stronger. But this view is not shared by all of our partners — notably the British government and even the French.

The third German position concerns the request of the Länder to influence European decisions both at the EC and the domestic level. The Committee of Regions has already been mentioned. But a second element which is not well known to the outside world is that the Council is no longer made up out of members of our national government: after Maastricht a Länder minister could speak for the whole country. It is clear that in the cultural and educational field, for example, the Länder will have a strong say in the EC. The same is true about our position on subsidiarity at Edinburgh. The various institutions and bodies in the Bundesrat and Bundestag keep the Länder well informed.

In the debate over Maastricht it has come clear that there is a certain fear about a too centralized Europe. The Germans say that if you want to have more power in Brussels we need at the same time decentralization — with more people involved and a balanced system of three levels of government. At the outset, it is important always to be informed about what is going on. It is true that the Commission is quite open, but we must know what is going on via the Brussels-based information bureaux of the Länder.

There are some elements of the Maastricht Treaty which help to go in the direction of a citizen's Europe — for example, the principle of subsidiarity, the increased power of the EP, the Parliamentary Ombudsman. Decisions should be taken as close as possible to the citizens — and that is not from the German point of view at the national level, but with regional and local authorities.

As far as Germany is concerned, the political side of Maastricht is too weak in comparison to EMU. The foreign policy-making competence of the EP should balance what has been achieved with EMU. Chancellor Kohl has said very often that we are only agreeing to give up our Mark if at the same time there is to be a political union. Here the Germans ask for a clear federal concept, and the principle of subsidiarity is one indicator of that concept. We could not achieve the federal words, but we do insist that taking decisions close to people is the most important part of subsidiarity.

Elderly Germans know when they are speaking of federalism that the principle of subsidiarity has been brought to Germany by the victorious powers. For example in Nordrhein Westfalen it was British officers who introduced the federal concept. Of course the intention was to use decentralisation to keep the Germans down, in political, military and economic terms. As a result Germany has a very complicated political system. The Länder have the quality of a state, with governments of their own, prime ministers and parliaments. There is a clear division of competences between Bonn and the Länder, giving the latter the say in education and culture, home and police affairs, and all matters dealing with the administrative implementation of national decisions.

The Bundesrat has the right to give its assent to all these laws, so the Länder have a very important say in their implementation. This is cooperative federalism, not traditional federalism. The Länder and the federal level have to work together in a cooperative way because both levels are responsible for the outcome. Very often the Bundestag and the Bundesrat have different positions but the constitution provides mechanisms to overcome those conflicts. In some cases the decision-making process is quite complicated, takes a long time and involves package deals in order to overcome the different positions. Acceptance of the political system by the citizens is eased by the inclusion of the opposition, either party or regional, in the resolution of these conflicts. People feel represented at either the one level or the other. It is, therefore, an irony of history that the federal system given to Germans to weaken them has proved to be quite successful in strengthening them. Moreover, the regional level is a good training field for politicians. It is often the case that national ministers or even Chancellors come from being a prime minister or minister at the Länder level — for example, Helmut Kohl and Willy Brandt. Regional politics gives the opposition the opportunity to get into the media.

In the economic field, there is a certain rivalry between Länder to attract investors, often with positive incentives, with the result that we do not have one big industrial centre like in France, around Paris, but a lot of industrial centres — Stuttgart, Munich, Hamburg and so on. So even in economic terms Germany is decentralised and this contributes to the strength of the economy. In societal questions, Germany's federal system means that we have great diversity in, for example, school policy. There is always scope, therefore, for comparison and even competition between the various regions.

Nevertheless, for all this, the tendency towards centralization still exists in Germany, as it does in Europe, and has to be countered. The EC Commission well knows that, despite the principle of subsidiarity, poorer countries, like Greece and Portugal, prefer to transfer responsibilities to the centre because somebody else will pay for them. Partly for this reason, there has always been discussion in Germany about the reform of the Länder. Some, like Hamburg, Bremen or Saarland have always been seen as being too small. The same could be said about Europe as well, for example, Luxembourg or Malta. In the EC smaller countries have a very important position in the Presidency, when in the case of Yugoslavia, Luxembourg, Denmark and Portugal formed the Troika. In my view, this was very dangerous for Europe. In the Bundesrat, on the other hand, the small Länder only have the duty of chairing the meetings, and other arrangements are made for important political negotiations.

There is in Germany a perennial criticism that federalism is too expensive. Do we really need 16 parliaments and governments? But this is an open discussion which helps the system remain transparent. All in all the majority of Germans are very content with the federal system. It is seen as a guarantee of balance by giving the opposition the opportunity to take part in political power. Parties like the Greens who in other countries are excluded from power, now have ministers in Hesse, for example.

My final thesis is that we Germans have a positive attitude towards federalism and we now want to transfer our experience to the European level. Our intention is not to give up power but to accept that the EC is an important framework for the solution of important problems, and, therefore, to influence EC decision-making in an active way. It is very important to dispel the feeling that there is Brussels and here we are, and we must prevent things happening there. Opinion polls show a broad readiness among citizens to accept joint decisions within the EC. In June 1992, for example, Eurobarometre showed 79% of Germans in favour of dealing with the Third World at the European level; protection of the environment 76%; scientific and technical research 72%; foreign policy making 70%; security and defence 61%. The critical question is currency, where only

45% are in favour of EC decision-making. Even the British public are ready to transfer competence in most of these fields.

Nobody in the Maastricht debate in Germany sees a danger that the nation state will wither away. On the contrary the states will continue to have a very important but not predominant position in the decision-making process. This will not be a classical federal system where competences are separated. It will be a new system of cooperative federalism. Although the Germans underline subsidiarity, this does not mean that the EC has no say in those fields where the principle applies. For us the principle is neutral. Subsidiarity has to be applied on a case by case basis. It is dynamic. It is a general concept applying not only to the division of·competences between the EC and the nation states but also subnationally. The Länder, especially, want a Europe of the Regions. We want allies — such as the Belgian communities — to support this idea. We are not losing our national and regional identities, but adding a new European dimension to them.

I end with two questions. First, how do we prevent the centralisation of power? Second, if we are going in the direction of a Europe of the Regions, how can we include those parts of countries where there is not a clearly defined regional structure? Here Spain, not Germany, is the interesting example.

Regions and Local Authorities in the Governance of Europe
by Paul Bongers and John Chatfield

Local Government's Constitutional Position
The constitutional position of local and regional government in an increasingly integrated Europe is now recognised as a vital issue in the subsidiarity debate. The Member States of the Community differ markedly in the extent to which they perceive the practice of government as a pooling of sovereignty from the lowest level upwards for the sake of achieving a broader common good. In some countries the local communities are regarded as the basic cells of society, whose autonomy is jealously guarded against encroachments by the higher levels of government to whom a part of their freedom has been surrendered. In these countries, national constitutions guarantee the principle of local self-government, and in many cases require special procedures to be observed before changes can be made to local or regional government structures.

In other countries, including the UK, the concept of the nation state is much more dominant, and local authorities, however deep their roots may go in some places, are perceived as owing their constitutional position and their functional responsibility to legislation enacted by the national parliament. Major changes to local governments's structures and basic legislation can be driven through parliament by straight majority vote without any requirement for special consideration of their constitutional implications. These differences of approach will inevitably have an effect on the way in which the different local government systems in the EC react to the constitutional implications of the Single Market.

There are also marked differences in the allocation of functions as between central, regional and local authorities in the various countries, with many moving towards greater devolution of power while a few are tending to impose greater limits on local autonomy. The creation of strong regional authorities has been a major political development in several European countries over the last 25 years. This has resulted from a combination of spreading power that was previously excessively centralised to the detriment of efficiency, and of providing scope for adequate expression of distinctive regional or national identities and cultures existing within one state. The strengths inherent in the German federal system (in whose establishment the British played a big part) have provided a striking example, and the Länder themselves have adopted a high political profile in recent years to campaign for a federal structure in the Community which respects and reflects their sovereignty.

What used not long ago to be considered starry-eyed talk of a 'Europe of the Regions' is now seen as a likely longer-term option for the future of the Community — although national governments will not loosen their grip on EC policy-making very readily, and some would argue that building a real 'Europe of the citizen' should be the first priority. However the European institutions have taken the assertion of regional identity very seriously, and the question of how it should be reflected in the development of the Community's structures shot rapidly up the political agenda in the early 1990s. Following its re-election, the Conservative government in the UK has continued to exclude the possibility of introducing regional government in England, for which the manifestos of the other main parties both provided, while leaving the door slightly open to some moves in that direction for Wales, Scotland and — circumstances permitting — Northern Ireland.

Meanwhile, EC policy trends and funding schemes have been powerful motivating factors in the development of regional groupings of local authorities in parts of England and in the emergence of the higher profile Assembly of Welsh Counties. The formation of the regions in Belgium, Italy, France and Spain has denoted a significant transfer of power from the centre and has been accompanied by some strengthening of the position and role of the intermediate authorities (especially of the départements in France) and of the municipalities. Local government reforms have tended to proceed piecemeal in an evolutionary way, with the mergers of municipalities, often fought over long and hard, being seen as the means of creating more viable units. Compulsion from the centre is usually very much a last resort. Root and branch reform as in the 1972 Local Government Act would be an alien concept in most other European countries. Incremental reform, as envisaged by the new Banham Commission, would seem to be a much more 'European' approach, whatever its detractors may fear about the uncertain situation of those authorities in the later phases of reform.

On the whole, continental municipalities tend to be smaller than British districts and more akin to our parishes in the rural areas, yet they are endowed with a substantial range of powers. Moreover, EC countries with strong local authorities often also have strong authorities at the upper level too, without apparently rocking the foundations of the state. British local authorities are rooted in a (still widely respected) tradition of sound public administration. They still have substantial executive responsibilities, and a large reservoir of in-house expertise at their disposal. However, they are increasingly seen by continental counterparts as being hamstrung in terms of real autonomy by the combination of the ultra vires rule and the constraints imposed upon them by the central government grant system. Pressures on local authorities from the national level during the rapid post-War development of the welfare state, coupled with progressive moves towards European collective action, had already led the leadership of the then Council of European Municipalities to assert the need for a European-level constitutional guarantee for the principles of local autonomy.

Steps Towards a Constitutional Guarantee
The first moves to do this in the Council of Europe were firmly rejected by national governments. But during the early 1980s the Standing Conference of Local and Regional Authorities of Europe formulated a new draft European Charter of Local Self-Government and succeeded in persuading the Committee of Ministers to adopt this, with some provisos, as the basis of a European Convention. This Charter was opened for signature in 1985 and came into force on 1 September 1988. It has now been ratified by 15 member countries of the Council of Europe and signed by a further four. (Extracts are reproduced in Appendix Two). The Charter sets out, in a flexible and adaptable format, the basic principles underlying a democratic local government system as the standard with which all pluralist democracies in Europe (and potentially beyond) should comply. The principles contained in this Charter now need to be considered urgently within the specific EC context.

Efforts to persuade the European Community to accede formally to the European Charter of Local Self-Government, obliging it to take it into account in formulating specific policies have so far been in vain. Whereas the Community has acceded to other Council of Europe agreements, it has been objected that acceptance of this Convention would be inappropriate since the Treaty of Rome does not confer any powers on the Community in relation to local self-government. Given, however, that more and more EC measures depend upon local and regional authorities for their implementation or enforcement, as recognised in the Maastricht Treaty's establishment of the Committee of the Regions, this objection would seem increasingly hard to sustain.

Initial Consultative Mechanisms
The institution of the Committee of the Regions in fact responds to one of the cardinal principles set out in the European Charter of Local Self-Government providing for the consultation of those directly concerned by legislative and

administrative measures about their formulation. Local government started campaigning for such consultation in the early 1960s, when the first effects of EEC membership were felt by local authorities in the original six member countries. With the formation of the European Regional Development Fund as part of the deal for UK accession to the Community, the pressure for a local and regional government voice at Community level increased significantly. Following a conference of presidents of regions and comparable institutions in Paris in 1976, the Council of European Municipalities (CEM), which subsequently added the Regions to its title in recognition of its broadening membership, and the International Union of Local Authorities (IULA), as the two representative associations then active at European level, jointly instituted their own Consultative Committee of Local and Regional Authorities of the Member Countries of the European Community. The motivation for this action was in part to influence the final shape of EC legislation and funding schemes impinging on the regions and, more generally, to impress upon the EC institutions that European unit should be built upon respect for local and regional identity and diversity.

Although initiated entirely by the local government organisations, this Consultative Committee obtained a degree of recognition from the European Commission. It began a real dialogue with the Commissioner for Regional Policy and with officials responsible for a number of related sectors including transport, social policy and public contracts. At the same time, the process of regionalisation in Europe had been gaining ground and, with encouragement from the Council of Europe, separate associations of regions with particular characteristics — such as the Conference of Peripheral Maritime Regions of the EC — were taking shape and clamouring for places at the negotiating table. Moves to bring the regional organisations, which had by then grouped themselves into a Council of European Regions, into active membership of the Consultative Committee were largely fruitless. But the Consultative Committee pressed on with efforts to obtain official recognition by the Commission as the representative voice for local and regional government.

The first Delors Commission, the launch of the Single Market programme and the accompanying proposals for doubling of the structural funds lent new urgency to the case for organised consultation with local and regional government. It became clear that, while official recognition of an existing informal body set up by the international associations could not be achieved, the Commission could establish more easily an advisory forum of its own. The Commission opened negotiations with CEMR/IULA and with what had by then become the Assembly of European Regions (AER) about the possible constitution of such a body. After lengthy negotiations about format and in particular about the respective positions of local authority and regional authority representatives, terms were finally agreed. The European Commission issued a formal Decision on 24 June 1988 setting up the Consultative Council of Regional and Local Authorities.

The Consultative Council of Regional and Local Authorities
The Consultative Council consists of 42 members holding elected office at regional or local level, appointed by the Commission for a three year term on the joint nomination of CEMR and AER. The members are divided between two sections, one representing regions and upper level authorities and the other representing local authorities. In practice, however, while these sections have played an active role in the selection of officeholders and have arranged preparatory policy discussions, most of the substantive work of the Consulative Council on EC issues has been carried out in plenary session, largely by consensus.

Like the other large countries, the UK has six places. It was agreed early on between the local authority associations that three of these should go to England (one nomination each from the Associations representing county councils, metropolitan authorities and district councils), and that one seat each should go to Wales, Scotland and Northern Ireland. While reflecting a broad regional balance, however, the UK delegates have seen themselves as a combined team representing UK local government as a whole rather than emphasising particular sectoral or regional viewpoints.

The Consultative Council held its inaugural meeting in December 1988 and has since met three or four times a year. Officially, its status is the same as that of many dozens of advisory groups set up by the Commission, but the fact that it is composed of leading elected local and regional politicians, nominated by their representative organisations, has given it in practice a rather different status and character.

The Consultative Council's terms of reference provide for it to be consulted by the Commission on any matter relating to regional development and in particular to the formulation and implementation of regional policy, including the regional and local implications of other EC policies. This provision has been interpreted quite broadly by both sides. As well as covering all aspects of the structural funds, the Consultative Council has given opinions on matters relating to the CAP, transport and environmental policies, social affairs, and support for local and regional democracy in Central and Eastern Europe. In the early days of this new forum, members reported that there was room for the development of more full-hearted consultation, as opposed to mere information sharing, by the European Commission. Through the dedicated chairmanship of Josef Hofmann, former Mayor of Mainz and President of CEMR, and then of Sir John Chatfield, former Chairman of the Local Government International Bureau and of the Association of County Councils, and with strong support from Commissioner Bruce Millan, a real policy dialogue was instituted.This has been invaluable in paving the way towards the Committee of the Regions. The Consultative Council is to remain in place until the new Committee is set up.
The Consultative Council's activities have highlighted the obligation that is placed upon its members, and the associations nominating them, to ensure that

they truly represent collective local and regional government opinion. Adequate mechanisms are needed at national level to establish such views, although on occasion national representative bodies have been unable to go beyond the valuable but limited role of reemphasising the essential purpose and right of local and regional authorities to represent diversity. Mechanisms have had to be developed, at EC level and within Member States, for a proper two-way flow of views between Consultative Council members and the authorities they are appointed to represent. This process is far form complete, and in some cases members have had no alternative but to view issues from the standpoint of their own region or local authority alone.

Significant steps are now being taken, however, in the UK and elsewhere to step up the capacity of the local authority associations to handle EC policy issues. This function is an integral part of the associations' policy analysis and representational role at national level — and should not be categorized as 'international' work of only exotic and marginal importance.

Input by the European Associations
The need to prepare local and regional government input into the Consultative Council and the future Committee of the Regions has also been a priority issue within CEMR and AER. This was a strong motivating factor in the 1990 merger which reconstituted CEMR as the Europe-wide representative body for national Associations of local and regional authorities, operating as the European regional section of the world-wide IULA. Since the merger, CEMR has been building up its direct presence in Brussels. It has streamlined its constitution and working structures, while developing a range of specialised committees to articulate European local government views across the whole range of relevant policy areas. There is now, therefore, a significant work programme on regional and urban policies, environment, social affairs and transport, and a continuing dialogue with the relevant Directorates-General of the Commission and the appropriate committees of the European Parliament. CEMR is currently considering ways and means of stepping up this work, but the limited resources available from membership income, the high cost of running meetings in and travelling to Brussels, restricts the scope of what can realistically be achieved.

The Assembly of European Regions is confronted with similar problems, but as a direct membership body open to regional authorities or other entities directly below central government level, it places lead responsibility for particular issues upon individual member-regions who organise the work on their own resources. At its best, this approach can be very effective. But inevitably the results are patchy, with some inconsistencies of style and approach. AER's leading member-regions are generally large organisations which devote significant amounts of resources to issues which they see as important. In principle, the member authorities represent only their own region, though some have a loyalty to one or other of the sectoral regional groupings out of which AER was formed. Issues of national balance may sometimes come to the fore. Thus the English counties, about half of which have joined AER with encouragement from the

Association of County Councils, seeing it as a useful meeting ground with authorities having similar functions in other EC countries and perhaps also as a source of support for County Councils in the British reorganisation debate, took concerted action in 1992 in order to obtain stronger British representation on the AER Bureau.

There is something of a dichotomy between AER's attachment to a 'Europe of the Regions' in which the German Länder, the Belgian regions and the Spanish autonomous communities serve as powerful role models, and its acceptance into membership of authorities in other countries which have quite weak powers and no comparable constitutional standing (and in some cases of regions which do not have even an elected assembly but are more in the mature of decentralised organs of the state). While some of AER's members are seen as component parts of local government, others control local government. The influence of the latter has tended to predominate in AER policy, with the effect that, while AER has generally worked in partnership with local government in the Consultative Council, it regularly takes up positions calling for a separate regional chamber at European level, with little more than a ritual bow towards the principle of consultation with cities and local authorities.

The Committee of the Regions

The confrontation of these differing positions came to a head during the Maastricht IGCs. The Treaty provides in Article 198 for the establishment of an advisory Committee of the Regions consisting of representatives of regional and local bodies. While it must be recognised that the German Länder and the other 'state regions' had a strong influence upon the Treaty negotiation process because of their extensive direct responsibilities for a range of domestic policies falling under the influence of the EC, there was a widespread recognition that the failure of the Treaty of Rome to acknowledge the role and responsibilities of local and regional authorities as part of the European democratic system needed to be put right. The new Committee was conceived, therefore, as running in parallel to the consultative forum already established by the Treaty of Rome to represent employers, employees and 'various interests' — the Economic and Social Committee (ECOSOC). This latter body, which many regard as unwieldy and not particularly cost-effective, has been taken as a constitutional model for the new Committee of the Regions in terms of the distribution of seats and the provision of consultation rights. The two Committees are to have a 'common organisational structure'. The new Committee will need to take care to establish its distinct identity and value in the early days of its existence.

Since the Maastricht Treaty was agreed, the issue of how its members should be appointed has been subject of intense interest in many EC countries. The organisations representing local and regional authorities had all emphasized before the Maastricht European Council in December 1991 that the new body must comprise elected representatives. The same point was made to UK Ministers by the Local Government International Bureau on behalf of the UK local authority Associations. The position was complicated by the fact that, when the Treaty came to be formally signed in Maastricht on 7 February 1992, the reference in the English text to 'regional and local authorities' had been changed to 'regional and local bodies'. (A similar change had been made in the Greek language version). This change was justified by the Foreign Office as representing a more accurate translation by the specialist jurists and linguists of the French and German terms *'collectivité locale'* and *'Gebietskorperschaften'*. This explanation was not particularly convincing — especially as the Secretaries of State for Wales and Scotland had intimated in the meanwhile that they or their officials might occupy seats on the Committee.

Throughout 1992 there was an orchestrated clamour on behalf of local and regional authorities for balanced representation within the Committee. Their argument was aided by the decisions of the Luxembourg and Danish governments. The 16 German Länder were, however, pushing to fill all 24 of the German places, and the 17 Spanish autonomous communities were laying claims to a minimum of 1 seat each. The three Belgian regions appeared to have convinced their Government that they should appoint all 12 Belgian places.

In July 1992 Sir John Chatfield, then Chairman of the Local Government International Bureau, set out a scheme for the division of the UK's 24 places between the various categories of local authorities in such a way that would provide geographical and political balance. The Associations undertook to come forward with an agreed list of names of representative councillors that would reflect the views of regional planning committees and regional groupings of local authorities. Requests for direct discussions with central government were rejected on the grounds that the Government was still considering the matter. Statements by the Secretary of State for Wales that local government was only one among several relevant 'interest groups' were not encouraging.

Gradually it became clear from various EC government decisions that a high proportion of the members of the Committee would be elected members of local or regional authorities and that the Committee when constituted would be seen by the Commission and Council as speaking for those authorities. By the time that the Maastricht Bill came back to the House of Commons following the first Danish referendum, local government was able to make a strong and united case for an amendment to provide that all UK nominees were to be drawn from councillors. Thanks to the support of a number of rebel Conservative MPs who saw this amendment as an opportunity to damage the chances of the Bill as a whole, the Government was defeated on this issue. The debate indicated that the principle of councillor representation was widely supported in Parliament. The Minister, Tristan Garel-Jones, conceded the point on 5 May 1993. Consequently, Councillor Charles Gray, Sir John Chatfield's successor at the Local Government International Bureau, submitted to Ministers a list of 48 councillors as the Associations' nominations to the Committee.

Meanwhile, in the Netherlands a number of Burgomasters and Queen's Commissioners, who are not elected but are clearly accepted in European circles as being "directly responsible to an elected local or regional assembly" and not as officials of the Dutch State, were appointed. The German Bundestag provided for 'at least three' of the 24 German places to be allocated to local government. This proportion was already considered wholly unsatisfactory by the local authority Associations, and in the Bundestag (composed, of course, of representatives of the Länder) the words 'at least' were deleted. In Greece, the Government announced its 12 members: alongside eight mayors, there were four 'regional officers' of central government, there being no elected regional tier of government. In France, the signs were that the previous Government would have allocated eight seats each to the regions, departments and communes, but the new government may be inclined to give more seats to the regions. In Italy, the political crisis has interrupted negotiations, and in Spain the competing the claims of the autonomous communities and the local authorities could not be resolved until after the national elections.

Considerable attention is being given to the future functioning of the Committee of the Regions. ECOSOC suggested an initial budget provision. They anticipated that the Committee would deliver some 50 Opinions in the first year, requiring a budget of the order of 23m Ecu and some 50 executive and secretarial staff plus appropriate interpretation and other support services, which will be shared with ECOSOC. For their part, CEMR and AER have been drafting possible rules of procedure for the new body. They want membership to be manageable by leading councillors who have existing heavy commitments. Clearly, the new Committee will need to work through small sub-committees (which in itself tends to undermine the argument that every region must have a seat on the Committee). The scope for involving experts and the provision to be made for CEMR, AER and party political groupings are also under consideration. It is hoped that CEMR and AER will arrive at a common approach to the rules of procedure, so that these may be endorsed at the inaugural meeting and forwarded promptly to the Council for approval.

In the UK, the local authority associations have agreed provision in the International Bureau's budget for a level of staff support to the Committee. The Bureau has also agreed that it and the Associations should ensure that advice to members is appropriate and well-coordinated. Clearly, officers of member's own authorities, officers of regional associations, networks of national Association advisers, and professional bodies will all wish to play a part in giving advice. The Local Government International Bureau is committed to facilitating the work of the UK members of this important new body which could make a significant contribution to reducing the democratic deficit in European Community affairs.

CHAPTER SIX

Subsidiarity and Scotland

Before the Edinburgh Council
by David Millar and Andrew Scott

By the time of the British Presidency of the Council of Ministers in the second half of 1992, reaching some agreement at the Edinburgh Summit on concrete steps to entrench the principle of subsidiarity in the context of European policy-making had become a priority objective of the British Government. That subsidiarity became a central theme of the Presidency reflects, in the main, the Government's attempts to allay the fears of many Britons, especially those within the Parliamentary Conservative Party, that Maastricht represented a quantum leap in the direction of a European 'superstate' in which some of the central functions of the nation state were to be passed to the European Commission to exercise on behalf of the peoples of the Community as a whole. The argument was that by entrenching the principle of subsidiarity within the Community process, this trend — should it appear — would be frustrated.

In this chapter we set out what we consider to be the salient issues at stake in the subsidiarity debate. In particular, we consider how this principle can be interpreted within the Scottish context, and how it can be utilised to inform the on-going debate on the subject of constitutional reform within Great Britain.[1]

Subsidiarity in the Treaty on European Union
There is no one satisfactory definition of the term subsidiarity. Like its counterpart term 'federalism', subsidiarity is open to a number of alternative definitions and interpretations. This explains, in part, why subsidiarity has achieved such an exalted position in the European debate and stems from the essentially different ways in which the term is used in the Treaty on European Union. Article 3b interprets subsidiarity as a procedural device that will determine the division of policy-making responsibilities between the nation state tier of government and the Community tier. Elsewhere, as in Article A, the central idea is advanced that subsidiarity should be a substantive principle that is to inform the constitutional development of the Community in the future. Similar wording appears in the Preamble, and Article B applies the principle. This is a different, though not inconsistent, deployment of the term in which the emphasis revolves around the substantive principle of democratic control.

Article 3b, on the other hand, applies the principle of subsidiarity to relations between national capitals and the Community level (although the basic point is applicable in delineating powers between any tier of government in a multi-level administration) and suggests that the Community should act "only in so far as the objectives of the proposed action cannot be sufficiently achieved by the Member States". Significantly, Article 3b is silent on the principle of subsidiarity as applied within the Member State.

It is worth recording that subsidiarity first appeared in the official vocabulary of the Community in Leo Tindemans's *Report on European Union* of June 1975 to the European Council.[2] In a passage which probably influenced the Institutional Committee of the European Parliament in drawing up its Draft Treaty on European Union from 1981-84, Tindemans foresees the application of subsidiarity:—

> "The need to ensure the political cohesion of the Union will probably mean vesting it with more extensive competences than those now exercised at European level. But, as in the Communities at present, the tasks assigned to the Union will be *only those which the Member States cannot effectively accomplish* . The areas of Union competence will be determined in its Act of Constitution, the others will still be attributed to the Member States."

The principle of subsidiarity found further expression in Article 12(2) of the 1984 Draft Treaty. Thence it was incorporated in the Single European Act in 1986. However, in that Act subsidiarity is advanced in the sense defined in Article 3b of the Maastricht Treaty rather than in the sense implied in Article A. As Wilke and Wallace (1990) record, subsidiarity in the Article 3b sense is clearly implicit in Article 130R of the SEA which states that "the Community shall take action relating to the environment to the extent to which the objectives ... can be attained better at Community level than at the level of individual member states". As we discuss below, this is a procedural rather than a substantive application of the notion of subsidiarity.

The Commission's View

In the Commission's Communication on Subsidiarity of October 1992, the proportionality and intensity of legislative action were analysed and guidelines for the application of these criteria of subsidiarity were offered.[3] Although the Commission insisted that the application of subsidiarity within a Member State was an internal matter and not one for the EC, the Commission indicated its awareness of the regional aspect of the application of subsidiarity. It stated that:—

> "In the Community context, subsidiarity means that the functions handed over to the Community are those which the Member States, *at the various levels of decision-making*, can no longer discharge satisfactorily. Any transfer of powers must have due regard for national identity *and the powers of the regions.*"[4]

The European Council at Edinburgh agreed an overall approach to the application by the Council of the subsidiarity principle and Article 3b of the Treaty which amounts to a distillation of the Communication by the Commission. Although the document states determinedly that the principle of subsidiarity "contributes to the respect for the national identities of Member States and safeguards their powers", it also "aims at decisions within the European Union being taken as closely as possible to the citizen".

The Edinburgh Annex specifically excludes from the application of subsidiarity the powers conferred upon the EC by the Treaty as interpreted by the Court, but provides a guide as to how these powers have to be exercised. It safeguards the *acquis communautaire*, the primacy of EC law and the provisions of the Treaty enabling the Union to acquire the means to attain its objectives.

Edinburgh defines subsidiarity as a dynamic concept, to be applied in the light of the objectives set out in the Treaties. As a 'fail safe' mechanism, it is stated that where EC action is excluded by the application of subsidiarity, Member States will still be required to conform with the general rules laid down in Article 5 of the Treaty of Rome by ensuring that they fulfil their Treaty obligations and by abstaining from actions which could jeopardise the attainment of the objectives of the Treaty.

One of the earliest criticisms to be levelled at the application of the principle of subsidiarity to the EC's legislative process was that it introduced substantial elements of imprecision and complexity which could serve further to hinder and obstruct the working of that process. The Edinburgh guidelines, procedures and practices to be followed in applying Article 3b cannot but delay the enactment of Commission proposals. Unless officials of the Commission, Parliament and Council are transferred from other duties to undertake the task of applying subsidiarity, new officials will have to be recruited in order to restrict such delays to the minimum. One palliative measure is however provided for in the Edinburgh Annex: to avoid lengthy discussion as to whether subsidiarity should or should not apply to any Commission proposal, the Council decision on this is to be taken at the same time as the decision on substance, and according to the voting requirements of the Treaty.

Subsidiarity: the Substantive Principle

To most people, the notion that decisions should be taken as close to the citizens as possible is a self-evident and fundamental pillar of democracy. Moreover, it is a notion that explicitly influences the federal structure of democratic government throughout the world. Inside the EC the principle of subsidiarity is most commonly associated with the German model of federal government. More recently, the newly autonomous communities of Spain have been held up as constitutional structures which embody the basic principle of subsidiarity.

The principle of subsidiarity in the governmental field is at present rarely applied, at least explicitly, inside the United Kingdom. The centralisation of decision-making in Whitehall and Westminster, or in the agencies thereof, is matched by the erosion of local autonomy by virtue of a continued process of reducing the powers of locally elected authorities. The proposed review of the local government structure in Scotland is widely perceived as representing yet another threat to local democracy.

The continued frustration of the popular demand for a Scottish Parliament is indicative of this general unwillingness to countenance the devolution of powers from the centre to lower tiers of government — those that are "as close as possible to the citizen". The current position is made all the more intolerable in the eyes of many people because subsidiarity evidently is a principle to which the British Government subscribes, the Prime Minister having been a signatory to the Treaty of European Union in which this principle has been most clearly set out.

If the principle of subsidiarity in what we describe as a substantive sense were to be applied to the government of the EC, the Community would evolve into a formal federal structure. In this way the danger of over-centralisation of powers at the centre in Brussels would be avoided. Of course, there are no concrete plans for the Community to evolve in this direction. More interesting is the proposition that the Preamble and Article A of the Maastricht Treaty provide a clear case for arguing that the principle of substantive subsidiarity should be applied within all Member States. Here the position of the UK government contrasts sharply with that of other governments. Excepting Ireland, the UK is generally acknowledged to be the most centralised state in the Community.

Procedural Subsidiarity: Re-defining Relations between Levels of Government — the 'Best-Level' Approach

As we have already implied, subsidiarity as it appears in the Maastricht Treaty has a second meaning — namely as a principle to determine the division of responsibilities between the EC-level and the nation state in areas of shared competence with the Member States. In this sense, subsidiarity is to be regarded as a criterion rather than a principle. Further, subsidiarity has to be interpreted within the dynamic context of an evolving Community propelled by the process of making 'ever-closer' the Union and committed to enlargement. In this sense, therefore, subsidiarity is a matter relating to the procedure for policy implementation through time. In this sense, subsidiarity says nothing about the objectives of common policies, or over what areas there should be EC competence. That is decided in the Council of Ministers. Instead, once it has been agreed that specific policy areas do require a common approach, subsidiarity will then guide the preparation and implementation of policy — such that the Community will act (in pursuit of the agreed objective) only in so far as this is the most effective means of achieving the end result.

In this respect, subsidiarity appears to be close in nature to other criteria that exercise a procedural influence over the integration process. One example is the criterion of proportionality, which is used by the Court of Justice when rendering a decision over some aspect of EC law. Proportionality refers to the notion that the instrument selected to achieve a particular objective should be proportional to the consequences that follow from that objective being attained. What this implies is that the Commission can be challenged in the Court on the basis that subsidiarity is not being observed in the implementation of a particular policy — despite the fact that the Commission may be working in an area in which it has shared or exclusive competence.

The meaning of subsidiarity in the procedural sense has much to do with efficiency in policy implementation. Accordingly, policy should be implemented by that level in the governmental structure capable of achieving the objectives of the policy most efficiently. Economists are familiar with this approach to assigning levels of policy to different tiers of authority in a multi-level government, having given it the title 'fiscal federalism'. In the context of the European Community, the MacDougall Report of 1977 remains the most important statement of this approach to determining the efficient division of responsibilities for economic policy arising from on-going integration. As economic integration deepens with the removal of barriers to the free movement of goods, services, capital and persons, the ability of a national government to achieve some of its objectives is weakened. Instead, the objective may be better achieved either by the coordinated action of all members of the Union, or by transferring responsibility for that policy to a higher level of government. There are many instances where this problem is being encountered within the EC at present — for example, in justice and home affairs. The risk is that co-operation between governments does take place, but that it does so outside the proper democratic process.

Subsidiarity: Principle versus Procedure

Demands that EC policy should conform to the substantive 'principle' of subsidiarity represent an attempt by subnational governments, principally the German Länder, to prevent an erosion of their present competences. In other words, the Länder are trying to buttress the elements of subsidiarity that already prevail within the German federal constitution. Similar concerns have been voiced by the autonomous communities in Spain. Here, there certainly appears to be a degree of tension between subsidiarity as a principle (the Preamble and Article A approach), and subsidiarity as a procedural device (as in Article 3b). On the one hand, the policy process has to be as close to the citizen as possible — which validates the Länder resistance to EC institutions usurping their constitutional position — while, on the other hand, it might be necessary that in order to achieve the objectives of the Union as a whole, some re-definition of relations between the different levels of government within the Union is required. This re-definition may cut across prevailing constitutional arrangements.

Thus, as the European Community moves towards an 'ever closer union', certain functions hitherto in the domain of regional and/or national authorities may need to be transferred to the higher level. For instance, the Single European Act regarded environmental policy as an issue which should be subject to some element of pan-EC regulation. This encroached on a policy area which had been the responsibility of the Länder, which caused some resentment. Similarly, if the EC moves to a common currency, monetary policy, hitherto one of the classical functions of the nation state, will be transferred to a 'higher' tier — the European Central Bank. Consequently, a comprehensive account of subsidiarity has to accept that, in some policy areas, further integration means that the EC-level of government will be required to exercise greater, rather than lesser, influence. In short, subsidiarity in the procedural sense implies a re-defining of the traditional role of the different levels or tiers of government, with some powers being passed down, and others being transferred up. This division of responsibilities between levels has to be based upon notions both of proportionality and of efficiency.

The tension between these two senses of subsidiarity may be reconciled in two ways. First, while efficiency is a key procedural criterion, the implementation of any policy cannot be done without regard to the democratic process. In particular, subsidiarity as a principle requires that the central tenets of representation, transparency and accountability in the policy process are reflected throughout the entire governmental apparatus — that is, at every tier in a multi-layered government. Should one institution or tier in the structure fail to reflect these tenets then the criterion of subsidiarity as a procedural device ensuring efficiency in policy delivery will no longer be applicable. In other words, if the policy fails to be legitimised by due democratic processes then achieving subsidiarity in the implementation of such a flawed policy will not resolve the issue. The problem lies not in procedural subsidiarity but with the failure to recognise subsidiarity in the substantive sense.

The nature of the present debate almost certainly reflects precisely this concern rather than any deep-seated hostility to changes in the policy-process itself. Hostility to the idea that the EC level of government should acquire 'greater' powers — and the use of the subsidiarity argument in Germany and Spain against this — appears to be rooted in the view that the EC institutions are inferior to national institutions in terms of the tenets of democratic government. Moreover, some consider that the EC has excessive power at present. This may reflect an inability for Community policy to react as required to reflect changes in the preferences of citizens — and this too reflects a lack of subsidiarity in the substantive sense in the Community's policy process.

This would suggest that what is needed if powers are to be re-defined between the subnational, national, and supranational levels — and for federalists this is an essential stage in the development of European union — is for the democratic processes surrounding the Community to be strengthened. Certainly this will involve enhancing the powers of the European Parliament and reducing the glaring imbalance in powers between it and the Council. After all, the Council is of little use to those countries that have a well-developed federal system as it has hitherto operated exclusively at the level of the nation state. This explains why the Maastricht Treaty provides for sub-national representatives to attend Council meetings (but only if those representatives have the power to sign agreements on behalf of their Member State). It also accounts for the creation in the Treaty of the Committee of the Regions.

The second mechanism for resolving the conflict between the substantive and the procedural approaches to subsidiarity is to provide for greater powers to be transferred to regional authorities. For if it can be demonstrated that regional authorities are able to implement even 'high level' common objectives it might be also efficient for them to do so. However, this requires that regions are able to formulate an inter-regional approach to achieving particular objectives. Coordination between regions is paramount. Regional cooperation would achieve both objectives of subsidiarity. It would conform to the need for policy to be made at the closest possible level to the citizen, and it would ensure that common objectives were being met by common actions. This would be the manifesto for the 'Europe of the Regions' which has been widely discussed in recent years. Maastricht paves the way for this pan-regional approach to Community government by providing for a Committee of the Regions, albeit that under the present provisions this Committee will have no effective powers. Indeed, a stronger case might be advanced for the introduction of a new Regional Chamber with a legislative function to sit alongside an enhanced European Parliament.

Almost certainly the practical compromise to resolving the subsidiarity question will be for the EC to follow a strategy that incorporates both these elements — enhancing democracy at the level of the Community institutions and involving the regions much more closely in the future shape of the Europe. Such a pragmatic approach would have important implications for Scotland.

Scotland in Europe - The Subsidiarity Dimension

We have already expressed the widely held opinion that the government of Scotland within the UK conforms to the principles neither of substantive nor of procedural subsidiarity. There are a number of policy areas over which regional authority has in the past been effectively exercised but which no longer fall within the remit of regional authorities. The delivery of local economic policies is one such area. It is straightforward to demonstrate that, on the basis of efficiency, local authorities are best placed to design and implement local economic policy. Despite this, the economic development functions of the Scottish regional authorities have, over the past twelve years, progressively been reduced.

The Commission considers that subsidiarity within Great Britain is a matter for the British people and not something for EC consideration. However, this may be a narrow view. There are a number of reasons why the prevailing constitutional settlement within the UK will act as a barrier to the UK's integration with the rest of the Community. How we conduct our internal affairs is therefore a legitimate matter of interest to our partners elsewhere in Europe.

In the first place, the structure of regional government in Britain is simply not equipped to play a part in any moves to establishing a Committee of European Regions that might, in the future, become a formal EC institution. The proposal in the Treaty of Maastricht is that the Committee of the Regions should be consultative only. However, in other parts of the Community, particularly in Germany and Spain, there is a groundswell of opinion arguing for the gradual accretion of greater powers for the Committee. As we suggested above, a powerful Committee of European regions or a new Regional Chamber is one way in which the governance of the Community could develop without raising fears that subsidiarity was being undermined. However, the present British government's resistance to devolving powers to regional assemblies within the UK is likely to be an obstacle to the development of a strong 'regional' representation in future EC development. The British government appears to be just as unwilling to cede authority 'downwards' within the UK as it is to cede it 'upwards' to the Community level. The UK, therefore, may block amendments to the Treaty which seek to give greater powers to Europe's regions.

Secondly, if nonetheless the Community does assign powers to the Committee of the Regions (or if a new legislative Regional Chamber is introduced by a reform of the Treaty), then the initial position of the UK government concerning representation on that Committee — delegating non-elected representatives of 'local bodies' — would have been problematic, and unacceptable in particular to the Länder as it would have diluted the capability of the Committee to cooperate to the extent required.

Thirdly, if the debate surrounding subsidiarity is resolved in a manner that favours the British approach — which is simply to decouple national policy from Brussels — there is a high risk that some of the important gains that have been made through present subsidiarity arrangements in Community policy will be lost. One important instance in which subsidiarity has already been practised is the operation of Community structural policy (for example, the regional development and social funds). An explicit requirement for access to EC funds from the structural budget is that regions, in conjunction with the social partners and national government, submit regional plans to the Commission detailing the arrangements whereby Community funds will be spent. Whilst this 'partnership' arrangement has not worked as well as was hoped, it does represent precisely the type of subsidiarity arrangement that could serve as a model for the implementation of other Community policies.

Fourthly, subsidiarity implies that responsibility is shared between tiers of government, and that each tier is responsible for those functions that it is best able to discharge. This means that the various tiers must be in continual contact through clearly defined institutional arrangements. In the UK there is no constitutionally entrenched provision for this. Regional authorities have little formal access to central government in the policy process. Ignoring the many questions about democracy raised by the British arrangement, there are practical consequences in terms of the formulation and implementation of policy. Where general objectives are agreed upon at the upper tier of government, implementation often becomes the responsibility of lower (national and subnational) tiers. It is important, therefore, that these lower tiers have the necessary competences to implement and monitor policy. In countries which have weak lower tiers this could well result in policy errors. It is clearly important to the Community as a whole that common policies can be implemented satisfactorily throughout its territory.

Finally, and significantly, the absence of a strong regional democratic structure in the UK is an obstacle to the influence that the British people can hope to play in the evolution of the 'ever closer Union'. UK citizens are less able to articulate their views 'from the bottom up' through representatives at local level who are able to ensure that local views are heard at Westminster and in the Community. As matters stand, EC citizens in Scotland are ill-equipped to make an effective contribution to the development of the Europe of the Regions.

What is clear is that the principle of subsidiarity can be applied to decision-making and policy implementation in the Member States as well as to the EC institutions. The degree to which national application will be possible must depend on the sophistication of the federal or regional structure in those Member States where it exists. Where it does not, a political will to apply subsidiarity must precede the introduction of structures for regional government. The realisation of such a political will is at present the task of those parties and groupings in Scotland which seek the introduction of a devolved system of government monitored by a democratically elected Parliament.

---

[1] The authors would like to thank Alan Lawson, William Paterson and Simon Bulmer for helpful comments on an earlier draft. They are, of course, absolved of any responsibility for the final product. The authors' views should not be attributed to the Europa Institute.
[2] EC Bulletin 6/1975 1101-03
[3] EC Bulletin10/1992 2.2.1.
[4] As above p118: authors' italics.

The Scottish Debate : three MPs debate subsidiarity on the eve of the Edinburgh Council

Alex Salmond MP, Scottish Nationalist

The concept of subsidiarity and the case study of Home Rule in Britain is becoming one of those things that habitually interest Europeans. It is a bit like the Schleswig-Holstein question of a few years ago: only three people understood it — and one was mad, one was dead and the other had forgotten it. I am not quite sure which category the Prime Minister fits into on the question of subsidiarity, but it occasionally feels like all three at the same time.

Clearly, I am rather more attracted to Article A of the Maastricht accord than to the fairly narrow definition in Article 3b. As a political principle subsidiarity has been heavily abused and debased over the last few months or so. It really is the central hypocrisy of the UK's attitude towards Maastricht and towards the Community to arrive at the position where subsidiarity starts in Brussels and ends at London. Certainly for a Prime Minister going to the capital city of Scotland to arrive at a definition of subsidiarity which excludes any notion about the people of Scotland having decisions brought closer to them is the central hypocrisy of the UK's presidency. There is an argument in Tory circles that subsidiarity within Britain is something to do with a strong central state, while subsidiarity is introduced via the Citizens' Charter. For most of us the definition would be somewhat different: subsidiarity is about empowering people to make decisions.

There is an interesting paradox in the debate about the European Community, seen from a Scottish and a UK perspective. There is no question that John Major feels the need to protect himself heavily against his backbenches because he believes it necessary to prove that the European Commission is going to be limited as much as possible. In other words the more limited Europe becomes, the more acceptable Europe might be. In the Palace of Westminster there are a large number of people who still operate on the assumption that Parliament is sovereign. So Europe and Maastricht are a threat to that power. The paradox is that, viewed from a Scottish perspective — and this is one of the reasons why the polls point to a much more amenable disposition towards the EC in Scotland than elsewhere in the UK — the removal of power from Westminster causes us very little anxiety whatsover. From my perspective the best possible constitutional position for Scotland within the EC is quite clear: that is as a Member State. And I would like to see subsidiarity applied as a concept within Scotland, as part of a developing European Community.

Now, why did the recent Scottish Constitutional Convention fail? The difficulty is that, while it is absolutely true that only 25% of people voted Conservative and 75% of people voted for parties who believed in and were in favour of some degree of Home Rule, it is also the case that on the Government's interpretation everybody who votes other than for the Scottish National Party votes for the Union and for the UK and therefore has to accept the UK result. So both Labour and Liberal Democrats are in the unfortunate, nasty and clumsy position that, according to the Government's interpretation, every vote cast for them as parties of the UK form part of the Tory mandate to govern Scotland against its will.

There are very few non-Tory people in Scotland who would share that particular opinion. Most people in Scotland believe that Scotland as a nation has the right of self-determination, but that of course the views of the other parties in the UK are of considerable importance.

In my view, therefore, the central reason for the failure of the Constitutional Convention is that it was predicated on the assumption that there would be a Government sympathetic towards Home Rule. And although the foundation documents of the Convention did not reflect that assumption — on the contrary, they were talking about challenging the sovereign right of the Westminster Parliament to rule Scotland — nonetheless most of its participants implicitly assumed that the way to implement the Constitutional Convention proposals was on the back of a Labour Party majority at Westminster. Take away that majority and you take away any hope or possibility of the Convention seeing for itself a role in post-election politics.

It speaks volumes for the Convention that it had its first post-election meeting on St Andrew's Day some seven months or so after polling day. But there is now a very stark choice for people in Scotland. For according to the Government's definition the only way we can register our belief in a new relationship for Scotland within the European Community is through a vote for national independence. Since the general election the SNP vote of 22% — not the 75% total non-Tory vote — has been used as the barometer of Scottish opinion. At Westminster there is a fairly considerable belief that the Scottish challenge has been seen off once again. I think that belief is wrong and that the challenge will re-emerge in much stronger form in the not too distant future.

In summary, therefore, my position is that the concept of subsidiarity should mean a great deal more than the UK government is willing to confer upon it. However, in the narrow definition of subsidiarity arrived at to suit the exigencies of Westminster politics, there is a very considerable danger that yet another opportunity to lead Europe forward to reconcile people's concerns is being lost.

Henry McLeish MP, Labour

Clearly this is a unique week for Scotland because we have the summit in Edinburgh, we have the government in difficulties on the Maastricht Bill, and we have a very significant BBC opinion poll about Scots's views of Europe. Out with the South East the Scots are embracing the Europe agenda much more than any other region in the UK, but, also, the Scots are very cynical about what that new Europe might provide for them.

The Scottish Constitutional Convention brings together in a unique sense a wide cross-section of political opinion in Scotland and many organisations including the churches and the trade union movement. There is a collective thrust in Scotland which has served us well over many decades, and is now alive in the Convention. But there are two organisations who will not join — the SNP and the Conservatives. Clearly, we understand the Conservatives — rooted in undiluted unionism and serving no interest in Scotland.

But the SNP's self-exclusion is a mystery to us. What we need in Scotland is a voice which will argue a way forward cogently and coherently. And, of course, the majority of Scots want devolution or Home Rule within the context of the UK. If you have undiluted nationalism on the one hand and undiluted unionism on the other, there is a massive distortion of the real interest of Scotland. Over the next two or three months the SNP might want to reconsider their position. Scottish interests would be better served by a unity which marginalised the Conservatives. But the current tragedy is the mutually reinforcing antagonism being developed between unionists and nationalists. Meanwhile, the government and Prime Minister thought that subsidiarity was a clever ruse to keep Brussels and Norman Tebbit at bay. In Scotland we take a much more vigorous and optimistic, radical view of what subsidiarity might hold for Scots.

Let me read to you a letter from the Prime Minister dated 3 December where, despite what he may say tomorrow, he states this about subsidiarity:—

"It is recognised that it is for each Member State to decide how its powers should be exercised domestically. The Community can only act where Members States have given it the power to do so in the Treaties establishing the European Community. It was for this reason that Article 3b of the Maastricht Treaty refers specifically and only to relations between the Community as a whole and individual Member States. It is up to individual Member States to order their own constitutional affairs at a national and sub-national level. What subsidiarity is not about is proliferation of tiers of government and bureaucracy".

This is dreadful and dispiriting. Clearly, this issue of the government 'taking stock' since the election is a sham. But if that is the case, why are we optimistic? It is not a matter of if Scotland has a Parliament. The only significant difficulty we have got to wrestle with is when. The British state in its current form is not tenable. Apart from the nationalist aspirations, we have the most over-

centralised, over-bureaucratised, insensitive and remote Conservative rule —
and, after 13 years, arrogant as well. That is not the basis upon which a
prosperous economy and a sense of democracy can be built. And I am quite
confident that the whole question of Europe and subsidiarity reinforces Scotland's
position.

There are two issues that will take Scotland forward: one is subsidiarity, and one
is the Committee of the Regions. Now, the Committee of the Regions is a very
modest concept, with very limited powers indeed, but it brings together the
notion that subsidiarity means devolving power to the citizen at the very lowest
level. The Committee for the first time allows elected representatives to be in
or around the heart of Europe, arguing forcibly for further developments on
subsidiarity but also giving a very powerful focus for our aspirations in the
Scottish community. Labour's objective is to ensure that the whole European
thrust of both these concepts will be further developed.

The Scots are by tradition internationalist in approach and fair-minded. We are
embracing the European agenda with issues like the Social Charter much more
than we are embracing the tired agenda from Westminster — which even
objectively has failed in relation to the objectives it set itself. Scots see in Europe
a tide of very positive change. In Germany, Spain and France autonomous
regions do have genuine powers, and they are concerned about influence being
lost to Brussels. We in Scotland are simply seeking to aspire modestly to that.

The Edinburgh Summit is not just the end of a disastrous Presidency, but the start
of a very vigorous campaign for Labour which will take Scottish aspirations in
new and much more imaginative directions. But Europe must respond positively,
too. Our partners should not be browbeaten by a Prime Minister who faces
enormous difficulties with his own party and country, and who will, through
Edinburgh, seek party advantage. A deepening Europe has to go forward
regardless of what we in Britain think — especially if we continue to constrain,
frustrate and in some respects humiliate our partners.

It is only by the European debate going forward that Scottish Home Rule will
be achieved. We have a very powerful combination of national aspirations going
back centuries, distinctive Scottishness, rich in culture and values, with a
collectivism you can find nowhere else in the UK. Europe is embracing the kind
of changes we want.

Jim Wallace MP, Liberal Democrat

With the European Summit in Edinburgh subsidiarity provides a focus for the
continuing campaign on Scottish Home Rule. The establishment of a Scottish
Parliament remains an unquestionable goal of my own Party. Indeed the policy

of Liberal Democrats is the ultimate establishment of a federal United Kingdom, although it has long been recognised that on the road there Scotland will inevitably take the lead. We believe that Scotland without a Parliament is a nation rich in talent but with her potential unfulfilled. Going back to the earliest years of the 18th Century, the Commissioners who were sent by the Scottish Parliament to negotiate the Union with England failed to honour their mandate when they did not return with a federal settlement. So today we find, possibly uniquely, a nation with its own legal system, a separate education system and church, and yet no domestic legislature to give expression to the nation's own political priorities. With powers increasingly being acquired by the EC the case for a Scottish Parliament — as was recognised almost 20 years ago in the Kilbrandon Royal Commission Report — is even more pressing in 1992 that it was in the mid 1970s, and certainly more so than when the Scottish Home Rule movement was founded at the turn of the Century by the Scottish Liberal Party. In our Liberal tradition we use the terms of Parliament and Home Rule rather than assembly and devolution. This is more than a semantic difference.

The Constitutional Convention established in 1989 played an important role in arguing the case for a Scottish Parliament. Little is known about the Convention south of the border. It was the product of a Claim of Right drawn up by some notable Scots in 1988. The very term 'claim of right' follows two historical precedents, in 1689 and 1842, when Scots acted against the misgovernment of their country. The founding declaration of the actual Convention acknowledged the "sovereign right of the Scottish people to determine the form of government best suited to their needs". Those steeped in English constitutional law will know of the distinction between the concept of popular sovereignty and Parliamentary sovereignty. Popular sovereignty allows for the development of government at different levels, and avoids some of the agonising which Conservative and some Labour backbenchers have grappled with over diluting UK Parliamentary sovereignty in the EC.

What the Convention has already done represents a remarkable achievement. It produced a comprehensive scheme of Home Rule agreed upon by many individuals and groups representing all walks of life in Scotland. The drawing in of people from different backgrounds has been of particular importance to my own Party because it has helped modify conventional politics in Scotland, and mirrors the purposes underlying the principle of subsidiarity. Subsidiarity is surely not only about having decision-making near the citizens but also about maximising the involvement of groups and institutions previously shut out of politics. Politics based upon cooperation and understanding rather than confrontation and misrepresentation is something identified with European not British politics. It has been a matter of regret to the Convention that the Scottish National Party did not join with us when the Convention was launched in 1989 nor come along since. The problem for the SNP is that, at an election which was argued on the basis of the union against independence, it only managed to acquire 22% of the vote. The Scottish people do not actually want independence.

Furthermore, the problem is not simply Scottish. It is a failure of the British system of government — a system that was over-centralised and undemocratic. In Scotland the injustice of the present electoral system is more pronounced, but we should not lose sight of the fact that in the UK as a whole 58% of those who voted at the last election are governed by a party to which they did not assent. The Constitutional Convention has shown a way ahead, and we must now try to mobilise opinions south of the border to help us in our task of fundamental constitutional reform. The Edinburgh Summit is an opportunity to do this. What is expected at the Summit is a statement clarifying what levels in the EC decisions are expected to be taken. Subsidiarity may not be a word which evokes unbridled passion. But the idea it conveys: that government should exist as close to the people as possible is, and for centuries has been, clear not just for Scotland but for other European countries as well. Pope Pius XI said: "It is an injustice a great evil and a disturbance of right order for a large and higher association to arrogate to itself functions which can be performed efficiently by smaller and lower societies". This is a fundamental principle of social philosophy, unshaken and unchangeable, and not a procedural concept.

Subsidiarity expresses fundamental perceptions about the way we are and wish to be governed. It ought to transcend everyday politics. It is a principle which in its application will give the people of Scotland the power to influence the public policy of our Scottish nation, and which should empower people in their diverse local communities and enable them to shape their own future.

Whilst in the preamble to the Treaty on European Union we have a very good definition of the principle of subsidiarity, in its procedural application in Article 3b it is technical and opaque. I suspect this is a tribute to the handiwork of John Major, who is wrong to insist that Westminster is the most appropriate level of government close to the people. And to try to argue that case in Edinburgh is breathtakingly insensitive.

Last year I had the advantage of visiting Catalonia and learning that the idea of subsidiarity and Home Rule are irrefutably connected not only with each other, but with the EC. In Spain, too, different provinces have achieved their own pace of self-government.

Scotland's right to her own Parliament is not just simply for the Scots. It is of crucial importance to the process of European integration. Subsidiarity will soon become the cornerstone of the Community which cannot exist without democracy at all levels of decision-making. While the European Parliament needs strengthening and Westminster's system is growing old, Scotland cries out for the rapid restoration of her own Parliament and an end to imposed minority rule. The Community's institutions will almost certainly develop to take account of the regional dimension. Britain's input must not be missing at this critical stage.

After the Edinburgh Council
by David Millar and Andrew Scott

The Edinburgh European Council took place on 11-12 December 1992. On the second day, a Saturday, a march for *Democracy in Scotland* was organised by the Scottish TUC. The three main opposition parties participated, alongside trade union delegations, and representatives of many other Scottish organisations. 25,000 people marched through the centre of Edinburgh to a rally at which a 'declaration on democracy' was acclaimed. It called for a Parliament for Scotland with power to oversee a Scottish government. The huge support given to the march, which was thought to be the largest in Edinburgh for fifty years, surprised everyone, including the organisers. But even at the rally differences between the party standpoints became clear: the SNP appeared to call for a boycott of Westminster by Scottish MPs, but this was refused by the other two parties.

Since the dramatic events of December 1992 several attempts to chart the way ahead for the opposition in Scotland have been made. The Labour Party backed an initiative by Campbell Christie, General Secretary of the Scottish TUC, to find a forum to replace the Scottish Constitutional Convention in which the SNP could participate. After weeks of discussion with the party leaders, Christie proposed that a Scottish Parliamentary Council should be created, comprising Scottish MPs, which would act as a "shadow Parliament", meeting in Scotland to hold debates and conduct enquiries, for example. This initiative won the support of the Scottish Liberal Democrats and the SNP but, rather curiously, was rejected by the Labour Party. At least for the present, Labour continues to espouse the Convention. However, further talks in London on 2 March between party leaders and the representatives of the Convention appear to have reached partial agreement. The Convention is to assume an educational rather than a campaigning role, although Labour continues to believe in the need for 'a new agenda'.

The three party leaders have now agreed to meet in order to seek a common strategy for wider constitutional reform. This would possibly be based on a campaign for a Scottish Parliament and a multi-option referendum in Scotland on the options of the status quo, devolution or independence. Meanwhile, speaking in London to a Charter 88 meeting on 1 March, John Smith, the Labour leader, confirmed that, if returned to power, the party would introduce a Scottish Parliament Bill within one year.

The government's promised White Paper *Scotland in the Union: a partnership for good* was published on 9 March 1993. The principal changes in the situation of Scotland within the Union relate to Parliament. The main instrument to be employed by the government to enable closer representation of Scottish interests in Parliament is the Scottish Grand Committee. It is composed of all MPs elected from Scottish constituencies, and has in recent years been comparatively little used. In future, Bills relating to Scotland will be referred to the Committee for a second reading "in principle", although provision remains for a formal vote or second reading on the floor of the House of Commons itself. This procedure will involve government Bills, law reform Bills and private Members' Bills. In addition Scottish statutory instruments requiring, or being the possible subject of, Parliamentary procedures will be debated in the Scottish Grand Committee.

At present the Committee is empowered to hold twelve debates on the Scottish Estimates, and on Scottish matters in each session. In future these twelve days will in addition include debates on reports from the Select Committee on Scottish Affairs on the allocation within Scotland of public expenditure. Oral Questions to the Secretary of State will also be taken on between four and six occasions and mini-debates may in addition be permitted on certain oral questions. The Scottish Grand Committee will hear oral statements by Scottish Ministers, who will also reply to short 'adjournment' debates on topics raised by Members. The Scottish Office Minister in the House of Lords will be available to give evidence to the Committee: this is a procedural innovation. For all these proceedings, the government have decided that the Committee could meet at Westminster, in Edinburgh, or elsewhere in Scotland.

After second reading, the Standing Orders of the House of Commons provide that a Bill may be referred to a 'Special Standing Committee' on legislation. Such a Committee may meet in select committee mode on up to four occasions over a period of 28 days to take oral evidence on the Bill. Thereafter, the usual line-by-line confrontational debate ensues. The value of the preliminary examination is that it enables interested parties to give their views on the more technical and detailed aspects of the Bill, which enables the Committee to debate it subsequently from a more informed standpoint. All in all, these reforms are to be welcomed as a means of enabling Scottish MPs to carry out their representative duties more effectively, within the limitations of the Westminster system.

Turning to the measures of administrative devolution, the government intend to devolve to the Scottish Office from London departments the control of training, the development of industrial innovation and technology, the management and operation of Highlands and Islands airports (at present run by a subsidiary of the Civil Aviation Authority), the Scottish Arts Council, and relocation of industry to Scotland. Many of these functions relate to EC policies.

In the realm of contact with citizens, the Scottish Office will open a central enquiry office and area information points in cities and towns in Scotland. The Citizens Charter and the Further and Higher Education Charter are to be further elaborated, and a guide to planning published for the citizen. The government maintains also that Local Enterprise Companies, School Boards and NHS Hospital trusts all serve to bring decision-making closer to the citizen. The White Paper states that "the Government are therefore committed to developing more decision-making not only to Scotland but within Scotland, too", and, furthermore that a "key theme for the future will be to place decision-taking closer to the point where services are delivered". It is stated that reform of local government is at the heart of this strategy.

On the face of it, this represents a major change of policy as it implies that at least some of the powers lost by local authorities since 1979 will be restored to them. The text of this section of the White Paper lays more emphasis, however, on local enterprise companies, School Boards, NHS trusts and membership of Quangos than on local government. And in turn the areas which are to be devolved from London, while useful, do not in sum amount to very much.

On 'Scotland in Europe', mention is made of the Committee of the Regions, of the Scotland Europa Office in Brussels, of Scottish Trade International (an agency for exporters set up in 1991), of links between Scotland and Bavaria, and of innovation work by Scottish Financial Enterprise. Scottish Ministers and officials will take part in more meetings of the Council of Ministers. On the Committee of the Regions, the White Paper states, "the Government will ensure that Scotland has substantial representation on it". It is notable that, as was made clear during the proceedings on the Maastricht Bill, the government had not intended such representation to be provided by elected local authority councillors. Moreover, when the UK's six extra seats to the European Parliament came to be allocated, Scotland (like Northern Ireland) received none. From June 1994, therefore, the new composition of MEPs will be 71 for England, 8 for Scotland, 5 for Wales and 3 for Northern Ireland.

CHAPTER SEVEN

The Reform of Local Government

The Banham Commission
by Malcolm Grant

It is an essential part of any discussion on subsidiarity that we include reference to local government and its reform, not just the work of the Banham Commission at the moment, but the whole process of adjustment that has been continuing since 1935, and has its contemporary manifestations in the problems of local government finance, the new arrangements for education, the transformation of housing and of social services.

The work of the Local Government Commission takes place against the background of enormous change in local government. We are charged with the responsibility of reviewing the structure of local government in England. Those of you with knowledge of the systems of Scotland and Wales will know that a separate process of review is taking place in those two countries, not involving a roving Commission. Our Commission is headed by Sir John Banham, a man who has intimate knowledge not only of British industry (as former Director-General at the CBI) but also of local government, having for years been the head of the Audit Commission. Twelve Commissioners were appointed by the Secretary of State following an interview by the Local Government Minister, to support John Banham in his function. The Commission is proving stoutly independent. Let me define independence, as I find myself a member of a quango, and unkind things have been said about the inability of quango members to think independently.

The omens are not good. First, since the appointment of the Commission is by the Secretary of State, there is an inherent risk of political bias. Second, we are required to conduct reviews as directed by the Secretary of State. Third, the Secretary of State issues guidance, and we are directed under section 14 of the Act to have regard to that guidance. There are two sets of guidance, one on procedures and one on policy. Although we are required to have regard to them, we do not have to follow them if there are good reasons for doing otherwise. We are restricted to a structural review, and the policy guidance indicates that one of the outcomes that the Secretary of State foresees is a significant increase in the number of unitary authorities. We have also responsibilities to look at boundaries, and in due course we become the Local Boundaries Commission.

Within these limits, the Commission is rapidly establishing its independence. This is possible for a number of reasons. We needed to establish independence from the outset in order to ensure credibility. We are certainly not placemen put there by the Secretary of State. The most important thing was to adopt a policy of complete openness. We adopted this policy at our first meeting, a willingness to talk to anybody about the work of the Commission, to be lobbied individually or collectively by groups that wanted to speak to us — both collectively as a Commission and also those nine executive Commissioners who are out in the field. The three 'non-executives', of which I am one, have accepted responsibility for particular policy areas including highways, transport and planning (which is the area allocated to me), education and community care. So there are policy reviews going on at the same time as regional reviews with the idea that the policy reviews will look at those areas which we think are of strategic importance and may raise issues that will transcend the boundaries of unitary authorities.

We have no hidden agenda. When we enter an area we will weigh up the alternative structural options, and we must listen to what local communities have to say. One major problem is reaching over the heads of local authorities. They clearly have views, sometimes entrenched views. Yet there has in some areas been a remarkable degree of convergence between authorities who only six months ago were fighting and seemed to have no area of common ground. They have now seen the great advantages of working together and working out a form of local government that can produce local accountability and a basis for subsidiarity. Although we are anxious to ensure that the people are also heard, that is extremely difficult as most people could not really care about the future structure of local government. You can reach over the heads of elected representatives but what can you hear? People are more concerned about specific aspects of local government performance than about the overall structure. People are often confused about which council is responsible for providing which service.

The criteria for the structural reviews are prescribed by statute, and it is useful to consider how far in accordance with these criteria the Commission can pursue the notion of subsidiarity through local government. There are two principle criteria. The first is that our recommendations must reflect the identities of local communities, and that raises as many questions as it answers. For example, what is a local community? People identify with different levels of community interest, at parish, city, county and even regional level. Some argue that in the era of the enabling authority, size no longer matters. The counter-argument is that, whilst we are seeking to create a sub-regional system of government, there is at least a need for units of local government that are strong enough and big enough to talk directly to Brussels and not be involved constantly in parish politics.

The second criterion by which we are required to evaluate options for change is that of trying to secure effective and convenient local government. This is contrasted with the necessity to ensure the reflection of local communities, and this implies that effective and convenient does not necessarily mean big. We then go through five different phases. First we look at each area at an initial stage which is an introduction and a solicitation of views from the local community.

We then write a report which is agreed by the Commission collectively. That is publicised, and we receive further representations from the local communities. We then produce a final report for the Secretary of State. The responsibility then rests with him to reject or accept our report, and to submit any necessary statutory instruments carrying them through to Parliament for approval by both Houses.

Let me identify what I see as being some of the difficulties with this procedure. First, it is a very limited process. We are talking about a process of structural review, but we have no power to reassess the allocation of functions between central and local government. We are faced with local government as it is now. Secondly, we have no power to review the distribution of power between existing local authorities and Parish Councillors. We can recommend that new Parish Councils be created, but if there is a history of bad relationships with Parish Councils it may be difficult to persuade the Commission that they are the answer to providing services and consultation for the future.
Thirdly, we are forced to have regard to things as they stand. We are not in a position to insist that a new unitary authority conduct its affairs in a particular way — for example by delegating, by agreeing to consult at parish level, or by establishing district systems for delivering services — whatever prospects are held out to us of such enlightened behaviour. We have no power to review the internal management of local authorities. The question has also arisen whether what is involved is simply a transfer of power from districts to counties or from counties to districts (which has led in many areas to competitions as to who is the most efficient deliverer of services at the moment); or whether the outcome will be wholly new authorities. The Secretary of State clearly has power, if he wishes, to follow the latter course rather than the former.

The fourth problem that we face is that many of those authorities which were county boroughs before the 1974 reforms are now tightly restricted by boundaries which would prove even more restrictive if they were to have unitary status — particularly for strategic planning functions. One answer would be to extend those boundaries out, but any attempt by the Commission to do this would elongate the programme by two years at least, and provoke fierce local opposition. Although we are empowered to recommend boundary alterations, we must understand these political realities.

To sum up, what has the local government review got to do with subsidiarity? It is a genuine attempt to review what system of local government best suits each area. It is not a dictat from Whitehall. It is a Commission going from area to area and listening to local opinion. It contains the seeds of a strengthened local government system, and a more sensitive local government system, more responsive to local needs. We do not accept the view that unitary authorities are a blueprint for the future. We envisage that there will be some areas where two-tier local government actually provides better services.

Elgar Jenkins, Conservative

Subsidiarity is largely seized upon at present in Britain by those who seek a weapon to fight off the encroaching power of another authority. Britain, in its argument with the Commission over which areas of the EC should exercise power, has grasped subsidiarity as an aid in its struggle. Local authorities, in their concerns both to strengthen their position against the power of central government and to secure a stronger voice in Europe, have also grasped the principle in aid of their efforts. How much will these develop a genuine desire to apply subsidiarity to British political life? Despite its successful application on the mainland of Europe, in Britain the jury is still out.

The roots of subsidiarity lie in ethical, social and political philosophy. It is a socio-political term, not a legal or constitutional principle. It has over time passed backwards and forwards between the fields of moral, political and social philosophy; been used in economic theory, management organisation and recently as a legal principle by the European Court of Justice. This could create uneasiness about its use by British Conservative politicians who in the main seek political, empirical solutions to problems. Its wide use could reflect, however, the strength of the idea.

The Conservative approach to Local Government is, in fact, in line with the essence of subsidiarity. I would give three examples to support this viewpoint:—

1. In the field of education policy, Conservatives are giving power back to the individual schools, teachers and parents as the best level to implement policy and moving power away from the importance of the Local Education Authority. As Conservatives we emphasise increasingly the enabling role of local authorities under which Councils decide the services they need to purchase and use a variety of providers to provide these services. In our concern to provide a more meaningful structure of local government we base our approach on the need for authorities to be based on identifiable local communities.

2. Subsidiarity suggests the role of Councils is to encourage, stimulate, regulate, supplement and complement, not replace, individual efforts. That is the Conservative way in local government. Subsidiarity carries the idea that responsibility for self realisation and support of others should lie primarily with the individual or, when the individual alone cannot meet those needs, within a family through voluntary bodies or private enterprise. As Conservatives we could not agree more strongly with that approach.

3. Finally, subsidiarity implies that Government should be at a level close to individuals. The approach to restructuring of local government has that at its heart. I hope that the Banham Commission will provide more unitary Councils in the shires in place of the current two-tier structure. These all-purpose authorities will bring all local authority powers to bear under one Council to

tackle local issues and would certainly be more readily understood by, and responded to, the needs of local residents.

The big question that might be put to us is this: surely if subsidiarity is applied to structures, then should there not be a regional tier between the local Council and central government? Would not a British Land better interpret the principle of subsidiarity in our country?

The Conservative view is "no". The essence of a government is that it must be an organisation with which people identify. In England there is absolutely no demand from local people for regional government and no strong identification with particular regions to provide such Councils. Attempts to propose such units are artificial and rest on no secure recognition in the hearts of people. People do identify with Somerset or Bath, with York and Yorkshire. They do not identify with a Western Region or a North East Region. Essex men and Essex women have come into existence but that is not a reflection of the people of Essex, rather the product of an advertising gimmick.

In Scotland and Wales there are national identities which the government has recognised by giving each a Secretary of State. Only a minority of the people of those areas want regional authorities for them. In 1979 a Scottish referendum gave the support for a national assembly from only one-third of those entitled to vote. At the 1992 general election it was economic issues that dominated the debate not regional government. As Conservatives we strongly support the Union. But clearly, if local people in Wales and Scotland were to show an undoubted majority for such a development, then the Conservative Party would have to reconsider the question. Even then we would question the need for the additional bureaucracy such a change would produce, the need for an additional tier of government and the high additional financial costs. (One estimate suggests regional councils might lead to extra spending of more than £4000m or 2p on income tax quite quickly.) Would all this be justified by improved government in these islands? Frankly we doubt it. The only way we can see possible development in England, Wales and Scotland is in the voluntary coming together of groups of local councils to consider together issues of common concern. There are such groupings to discuss economic development questions and future structure planning. There is, however, a world of difference between such voluntary groupings arising out of a natural development and ones imposed from above.

Conservatives are passionate believers in local government, but our message is that there is much work for all of us in governing well in those areas where government is needed and exists rather than seeking to invent new layers of government — whether under the cry of 'subsidiarity' or any other clarion call.

Jeremy Beecham, Labour

It is a commentary on the Prime Minister's underdeveloped sense of irony that he took the summit to Edinburgh in the first place. A conference which deals with subsidiarity, which has as part of the Treaty under discussion a Committee of the Regions, meeting in Scotland of all places, strikes me as a curious choice of venue. Moreover, the whole of local government agrees with that it is intolerable to suggest that the Committee of the Regions in this country alone of the countries of Europe is made up otherwise than from elected members.

The general pattern within Europe has been of successful regional government, in the German Länder, the Italian regions, the provinces in Spain and France. On the whole they have got a rather better record of economic and social progress than we have enjoyed in this country. I know, for example, a small striking statistic: in Italy the province of Emilia-Romagnia does more in R&D than the DTI does for the whole of the UK, and the small business sector in that part of Italy is indeed thriving, and at any rate contributes to the success of Italian manufacturing industry.

In this country we do not have to create regional government. We already have it — an invisible regional government by civil servants and by quangos. It is not elected; it is not accountable except to the central government of the day. It is there in the fields of health and economic policy, and in branches of government departments as diverse as regional sports councils — a whole raft of 'governmenting' carried on at regional level but not by or through elected representatives. Indeed with the development of the so-called Next Steps Agency, parliamentary accountability is being diluted as effectively and thoroughly as local accountability.

So if we have regional government, it needs to be part of the democratic process. That is where subsidiarity comes in — the notion being that some of the functions exercised by national government should be brought down to a regional level. This is particularly attractive in the context of Europe, because we in this country have seen the manipulation of European funds by central government. That is not just a matter of the Conservative government but the previous Labour government as well. Both parties distort the concept of additionality and collar (increasingly in the last few years) EC funding for central government projects. The peripheral regions in this country are disadvantaged in the competition for European funding because they do not have the direct access to the Commission of some of our EC competitors. Since we are not in the 'Golden Triangle' or 'Blue Banana', most regions in this country find themselves at a disadvantage. An important role of a regional structure would be to allow direct access of directly-elected local or regional government into the European machine.

There is a further series of functions which could be carried out at regional level, largely drawn from central government — the functions of Regional Health Authorities, the Department of Transport at regional level, public utility watchdog bodies and a variety of similar things. There are one or two local government functions which might be appropriate to move up, but essentially it would be a devolution down from the centre.

The development of regionalism is to be seen not merely in a British context in the current EC, but looking further East in Europe it appears to offer a way forward from narrow nationalism. Historic antipathy of one people against another tends to be protracted into a demand for fully-fledged independent states with all accoutrements, whereas a more balanced regional structure with a substantial amount of devolution does seem to be a better way forward. In some ways, therefore, it is almost a case of Western Europe setting an example to Eastern Europe in how to manage their current conflicts. In the UK, however, and contrary to the trend in Europe, the last few years have seen an enormous tide of centralism. Quite apart from the financial controls on local government — capping budgets, curtailing capital programmes and restricting use of the receipts from the sale of capital assets — functions have been stripped away in water, health, further education and the careers services, and, soon in secondary and primary education as well. We have seen in the deregulation of transport, compulsory competitive tendering, urban development corporations and TECs, the role of local authorities diminishing substantially. There is now a question mark about the future of police authorities and the fire service, with the Home Office — never known as an enthusiastic participant in any interdepartmental initiative or able to work with local government wholeheartedly — already taking a concerted interest in possibilities there.

The government's view is minimalist when it comes to the management of local authority functions. What they see is a bundle of functions to be provided somehow, with local authorities being responsible for the competitive bidding process. What is missing from that is a recognition of the strategic and representative role of local government, as well as the notion of direct accountability. This really flies in the face of much of European political thinking as explained in the *European Charter of Self-Government* , which is in itself a very telling phrase from which British governments have recoiled. Local self-government is not on the agenda in Britain. It ought to be. That really is what subsidiarity in this country means.

The application of the principle of subsidiarity would not only provide in an accountable way the services needed by individual communities, but also would influence better the development of national and international policy. Europe is not simply a question of the ERDF and ESF and so on. Local government must not fall into the trap of simply being concerned with access to these financial resources. We must be in a position to influence EC policy directives which not only effect local government as an institution but which effect local communities. Again a regional structure would assist.

The appointment of the Banham Commission struck me as rather like the 'City

Challenge', where we were all invited to bid without any idea of what the criteria were. The choices had been made in advance and the reasons would be supplied later. The whole basis of the review seems to be fundamentally flawed because you cannot determine what are the appropriate structures for local government, never mind what are its boundaries, while not knowing what functions it is going to be exercising. There is simply no consensus between local and central government about this issue. The work of the Banham Commission may as well be written on sand unless within the next year or two that consensus actually develops.

The predilection for unitary authorities is right, however. Perhaps the claims to unitary status of what used to be the major county boroughs, with the big cities acquiring metropolitan status, will emerge from this process. But we must avoid one of the potential traps of creating small authorities, and end up with the stripping out of local government functions by the centre. For it can be argued that a small unitary authority for Weardale, for example, cannot function as an education or social services authority. This may not be an argument for not creating Weardale, but will be an argument used by some for not leaving these functions in the hands of local government. That danger can be avoided if the new authorities are of a reasonable size. You do not have to lay down a particular figure, but the process is starting with a 60,000 unitary authority in the Isle of Wight. The important thing is that the structure should be capable of carrying out the functions of local self-government both in its representative and in its service delivery role.

With that as the basic structure of local government — with the regional tier bringing from the centre what can be done effectively and accountably at a regional level — we will have a modernised system of government in this country which would echo the increasingly successful experience of, and allow us to deal on equal terms with, our European partners.

Andrew Stunell, Liberal Democrat

I want to ask a fundamental question. Is anything wrong? Do we need a review? The basic problem with local democracy in this country is that it does not have 'subsidiarity' in relation to central government. We have seen over several decades an increasing power of centralisation and control of local democracy. The review will not have any effect at all on the transfer of powers from local democracy. Indeed there is nothing to prevent the government during the period of the review taking more powers away if it wishes to, without any reference to the Banham Commission or anybody else. There is nothing to prevent central government imposing more stringent financial controls on to local government if it chooses to do so. We are the only EC country which does not have a constitutionally entrenched local democracy. Here it is seen as simply an adjunct of central government, or seen very much in the context of a system which gives all power to the 'Queen in Parliament' — which in fact means to the First Lord of the Treasury, the Prime Minister. I reject that model completely. We ought to be establishing in this country a plural democracy with an independent legitimate existence for local government entrenched in our constitution and incapable of being destroyed by central government. A second important point is to recognise that you cannot destroy power and you cannot create power, you can only redistribute it. A lot of the current arguments between Britain and the EC, and for that matter between counties and the districts, is about redistributing power. What we should be aiming for is a democratic constitutional system which stretches right the way from the local neighbourhood parish through to Brussels and perhaps ultimately beyond that. Every level of that democracy should be accountable — not to Parliament but to the people, to the community served by those local authorities. The idea of using the sovereignty of Parliament as the judge of what should or should not happen with local democracy is fundamentally flawed.

It is also ephemeral and illusory, because Parliament does not even exercise effective control over quangos or ministers. We have a business culture, where power is exercised by people running things on business principles and not on democratic principles. It is actually seen as an advantage if decisions are taken in a business-like way rather than taking account of local democracy or for that matter national democracy.

We should have a system which passes power continually back to the people that should have it in the local communities. We ought to judge what we do with power on the basis of what it will bring to the people affected by it rather than the benefits to those who exercise it. We do need a European level of democracy, a national level of democracy, a regional level of democracy and a local level of democracy. The principle which decides how we structure that, and which functions and responsibilities are taken by which level, is, I suppose, what is meant by subsidiarity.

It clearly is not sensible for a parish council to be responsible for deciding the motorway line between London and Newcastle; it is no longer sensible for Britain to be responsible for the problems in the Balkans where, perhaps 100 years ago, Mr Gladstone really was. It is not actually possible for an organisation like the EC to sort out the GATT agreement. There are different decisions which need to be dealt with at increasingly higher global levels.

There is a need in the British constitutional system both for an enhanced lower level of democracy in terms of parishes and neighbourhoods and an enhanced regional level. In both cases the right formula is to pull powers down and not to push powers up from levels below. In the UK, there is no need for any local government function to be exercised by the regions. In fact I think that even some government functions currently exercised by unelected regional bodies do not need to go to regional government but need to come back to local government. If the Scandanavian countries can run their national health service from the county level, I do not see any reason why we should not be looking at that for this country.

What worries me is that rigidity on the question of devolution in an immobile, fixed constitution will lead to a moment when there is a catastrophic break, just as there has been in Eastern Europe. Immobility will lead to fragmentation. What I would prefer is evolution leading to devolution, not revolution leading to anarchy. Democracy is not just about providing services. It is about representing people. It is a sad fact that central government believes that 'representation of the people' is the least important. They have done everything they can to restrict what local government can do by restricting its freedom to take any action on behalf of the general public which is not service-based.

Yet the principal political event has been the government exercising its *representative* role in relation to the other EC leaders in Edinburgh. It is not about service delivery by the British Government or civil service. The European Council is about representing people — the most important job — and Edinburgh ought to recognise that as the fundamental job of local democracy too. That is why I recommend to the Banham Commission that a first step should be the setting up of a comprehensive tier of community councils throughout this country, including the urban areas in London, where at the moment it is illegal to do so.

That representative function is extremely important, and if we are going to have in the future unitary authorities which are the size of the old county boroughs (200,000 or more people), then that is not 'close enough to the people' to ensure that there is adequate community representation. There should be a much greater reflection of natural community boundaries. It is not just a question of administrative convenience, it is a question of natural communities, and I hope the Banham Commission will look very flexibly at what can be done on that.

There should be regional authorities. It is a sensible step forward as it is a way of coordinating regional and local action to the benefit of the whole area. Regions are going to be a useful tool in developing the economy, and in developing the sense of belonging to a United Kingdom. But an independent and plural democracy needs an independent source of finance. Clearly you cannot have a plural democracy when 85% of the money is doled out by central government. Here, too, is a fundamental underlying reform which has to be accomplished.

The Edinburgh Annex

Annex to the Conclusions of the Presidency of the European Council at Edinburgh 11-12 December 1992

Part One: Overall Approach to the Application by the Council
of the Subsidiarity Principle
and Article 3b of The Treaty On European Union

I. Basic Principles

European Union rests on the principle of subsidiarity, as is made clear in Articles A and B of the Treaty on European Union. This principle contributes to the respect for the national identities of Member States and safeguards their powers. It aims at decisions within the European Union being taken closely as possible to the citizen.

1. Article 3b of the EC Treaty covers three main elements:—

— a strict limit on the Community action (first paragraph);
— a rule (second paragraph) to answer the question 'Should the Community act?'. This applies to areas which do not fall within the Community's exclusive competence;
— a rule (third paragraph) to answer the question: 'What should be the intensity or nature of the Community's action?'. This applies whether or not the action is within the Community's exclusive competence.

2. The three paragraphs cover three distinct legal concepts which have historical antecedents in existing Community Treaties or in the case-law of the Court of Justice:—

(i) The principle that the Community can only act where given the power to do so — implying that national powers are the rule and the Community's the exception — has always been a basic feature of the Community legal order (the principle of attribution of powers).

(ii) The principle that the Community should only take action where an objective can better be attained at the level of the Community than at the level of the individual Member States is present in embryonic or implicit form in some provisions of the ECSC Treaty and the EEC Treaty; the Single European Act spelled out the principle in the environment field (the principle of subsidiarity in the strict legal sense).

(iii) The principle that the means to be employed by the Community should be proportional to the objective pursued is the subject of a well-established case-law of the Court of Justice which, however, has been limited in scope and developed without the support of a specific article in the Treaty (the principle of proportionality or intensity).

3. The Treaty on European Union defines these principles in explicit terms and gives them a new legal significance:—

— by setting them out in the Article 3b as general principles of Community law;
— by setting out the principle of subsidiarity as a basic principle of the European Union;[1]
— by reflecting the idea of subsidiarity in the drafting of several new Treaty articles.[2]

4. The implementation of Article 3b should respect the following basic principles:—

— Making the principle of subsidiarity and Article 3b work is an obligation for all the Community institutions, without affecting the balance between them. An agreement shall be sought to this effect between the European Parliament, the Council and the Commission, in the framework of the interinstitutional dialogue which is taking place among these institutions.

— The principle of subsidiarity does not relate to and cannot call into question the powers conferred on the European Community by the Treaty as interpreted by the Court. It provides a guide as to how those powers are to be exercised at the Community level, including in the application of Article 235. The application of the principle shall respect the general provisions of the Maastricht Treaty, including the "maintaining in full of the *acquis communautaire*", and it shall not affect the primacy of Community law nor shall it call into question the principle set out in Article F(3) of the Treaty on European Union, according to which the Union shall provide itself with the means necessary to attain its objectives and carry through its policies.

— Subsidiarity is a dynamic concept and should be applied in the light of the objectives set out in the Treaty. It allows Community action to be expanded where circumstances so require, and conversely, to be restricted or discontinued where it is no longer justified.

— Where the application of the subsidiarity test excludes Community action, Member States would still be required in their action to comply with the general rules laid down in Article 5 of the Treaty, by taking all appropriate measures to ensure fulfilment of their obligations under the Treaty and by abstaining from any measure which could jeopardize the attainment of the objectives of the Treaty.

— The principle of subsidiarity cannot be regarded as having direct effect; however, interpretation of this principle, as well as review of compliance with it by the Community institutions are subject to control by the Court of Justice, as far as matters falling within the Treaty establishing the European Community are concerned.

— Paragraphs 2 and 3 of Article 3b apply only to the extent that the Treaty gives to the institution concerned the choice whether to act and/or a choice as to the nature and extent of the action. The more specific the nature of a Treaty requirement, the less scope exists for applying subsidiarity. The Treaty imposes a number of specific obligations upon the Community institutions, for example concerning the implementation and enforcement of Community law, competition policy and the protection of Community funds. These obligations are not affected by Article 3b: in particular the principle of subsidiarity cannot reduce the need for Community measures to contain adequate provision for the Commission and the Member States to ensure that Community law is properly enforced and to fulfil their obligations to safeguard Community expenditures.

— Where the Community acts in an area falling under shared powers the type of measures to apply has to be decided on a case by case basis in the light of the relevant provisions of the Treaty.[3]

II. Guidelines

In compliance with the basic principles set out above, the following guidelines — specific to each paragraph of Article 3b — should be used in examining whether a proposal for a Community measure conforms to the provisions of Article 3b.

First paragraph (Limit on Community action)

Compliance with the criteria laid down in this paragraph is a condition for any Community action.

In order to apply this paragraph correctly the institutions need to be satisfied that the proposed action is within the limits of the powers conferred by the Treaty and is aimed at meeting one or more of its objectives. The examination of the draft measure should establish the objective to be achieved and whether it can be justified in relation to an objective of the Treaty and that the necessary legal basis for its adoption exists.

Second paragraph (Should the Community act?)

(i) This paragraph does not apply to matters falling within the Community's exclusive competence.

For Community action to be justified the Council must be satisfied that both aspects of the subsidiarity criterion are met: the objectives of the proposed action cannot be sufficiently achieved by Member States' action and they can therefore be better achieved by action on the part of the Community.

(ii) The following guidelines should be used in examining whether the above-mentioned condition is fulfilled:—

— the issue under consideration has transnational aspects which cannot be satisfactorily regulated by action by Member States; and/or

— actions by Member States alone or lack of Community action would conflict with the requirements of the Treaty (such as the need to correct distortion of competition or avoid disguised restrictions on trade or strengthen economic and social cohesion) or would otherwise significantly damage Member States' interests; and/or

— the Council must be satisfied that action at Community level would produce clear benefits by reason of its scale or effects compared with action at the level of the Member States.

(iii) The Community should only take action involving harmonisation of national legislation, norms or standards where this is necessary to achieve the objectives of the Treaty.

(iv) The objective of presenting a single position of the Member States vis-à-vis third countries is not in itself a justification for internal Community action in the area concerned.

(v) The reasons for concluding that a Community objective cannot be sufficiently achieved by the Member States but can be better achieved by the Community must be substantiated by qualitative or, wherever possible, quantitative indicators.

Third paragraph (*Nature and extent of Community action*)

(i) This paragraph applies to all Community action, whether or not within exclusive competence.

(ii) Any burdens, whether financial or administrative, falling upon the Community, national governments, local authorities, economic operators and citizens, should be minimised and should be proportionate to the objective to be achieved;

(iii) Community measures should leave as much scope for national decision as possible, consistent with securing the aim of the measure and observing the requirements of the Treaty. While respecting Community law, care should be taken to respect well-established national arrangements and the organisation and working of Member States' legal systems. Where appropriate and subject to the need for proper enforcement, Community measures should provide Member States with alternative ways to achieve the objectives of the measures.

(iv) Where it is necessary to set standards at Community level, consideration should be given to setting minimum standards, with freedom for Member States to set higher national standards, not only in the areas where the Treaty so requires (118a, 130t) but also in other areas where this would not conflict with the objectives of the proposed measure or with the Treaty.

(v) The form of action should be as simple as possible, consistent with satisfactory achievement of the objective of the measure and the need for effective enforcement. The Community should legislate only to the extent necessary. Other things being equal, directives should be preferred to regulations and framework directives to detailed measures. Non-binding measures such as recommendations should be preferred where appropriate. Consideration should also be given where appropriate to the use of voluntary codes of conduct.

(vi) Where appropriate under the Treaty, and provided this is sufficient to achieve its objectives, preference in choosing the type of Community action should be given to encouraging cooperation between Member States, coordinating national action or to complementing, supplementing or supporting such action.

(vii) Where difficulties are localised and only certain Member States are affected, any necessary Community action should not be extended to other Member States unless this is necessary to achieve an objective of the Treaty.

III. Procedures and Practices

The Treaty on European Union obliges all institutions to consider, when examining a Community measure, whether the provisions of Article 3b are observed.

For this purpose, the following procedures and practices will be applied in the framework of the future of the basic principles set out under section II and without prejudice to a future interinstitutional agreement.

(a) The Commission

The Commission has a crucial role to play in the effective implementation of Article 3b, given its right of initiative under the Treaty, which is not called into question by the application of this article.

The Commission has indicated that it will consult more widely before proposing legislation, which could include consultation with all the Member States and a more systematic use of consultation documents (green papers). Consultation could include the subsidiarity aspects of a proposal. The Commission has also made it clear that, from now on and according to the procedure it already established in accordance with the commitment taken at the European Council in Lisbon, it will justify in a recital the relevance of its initiative with regard to the principle of subsidiarity. Whenever necessary, the explanatory memorandum accompanying the proposal will give details on the considerations of the Commission in the context of Article 3b.

The overall monitoring by the Commission of the observance of the provisions of Article 3b in all its activities is essential and measures have been taken by the Commission in this respect. The Commission will submit an annual report to the European Council and the European Parliament through the General Affairs Council on the application of the Treaty in this area. This report will be of value in the debate on the annual report which the European Council has to submit to the European Parliament on progress achieved by the Union (see Article D in the Treaty on European Union).

(b) The Council

The following procedure will be applied by the Council from the entry into force of the Treaty. In the meantime they will guide the work of the Council.

The examination of the compliance of a measure with the provisions of Article 3b should be undertaken on a regular basis; it should become an integral part of the overall examination of any Commission proposal and be based on the substance of the proposal. The relevant existing Council rules, including those on voting, apply to such examination.[4] This examination includes the Council's own evaluation of whether the Commission proposal is totally or partially in conformity with the provisions of Article 3b (taking as a starting point for the examination the Commission's recital and explanatory memorandum) and whether any change in the proposal envisaged by the Council is in conformity with those provisions. The Council decision on the subsidiarity aspects shall be taken at the same time as the decision on substance and according to the voting requirements set out in the Treaty. Care should be taken not to impede decision-making in the Council and to avoid a system of preliminary or parallel decision-making.

The Article 3b examination and debate will take place in the Council responsible for dealing with the matter. The General Affairs Council will have responsibility for general questions relating to the application of Article 3b. In this context the General Affairs Council will accompany the annual report from the Commission (see 2(a) above) with any appropriate considerations on the application of this Article by the Council.

Various practical steps to ensure the effectiveness of the Article 3b examination will be put into effect including:—

—   working group reports and COREPER reports on a given proposal will, where appropriate, describe how Article 3b has been applied;

—   in all cases of implementation of the Article 189b and 189c procedure, the European Parliament will be fully informed of the Council's position concerning the observance of Article 3b, in the explanatory memorandum which the Council has to produce according to the provisions of the Treaty. The Council will likewise inform the Parliament if it partially or totally rejects a Commission proposal on the ground that it does not comply with the principle of Article 3b.

Part Two: Subsidiarity — Examples of the Review of Pending Proposals and Exisiting Legislation

The Birmingham European Council agreed that, to flesh out the subsidiarity principle, it would examine at Edinburgh the initial outcome of a Commission review of existing Community legislation, with examples.

The Commission has proceeded along three lines:—

◆ in October it gave the other institutions the fruits of its reflections on subsidiarity in the form of a political, technical and legal analysis;

◆ it proposed broad lines for an interinstitutional agreement, which were substantially accepted by Parliament and well received by Member States. The subsidiarity principle has an impact on all the three institutions involved in their respective ways in the decision-making and legislative process;

◆ the Commission, for its part, embarked on a review of pending proposals, an initial analysis of exisiting legislation, and deeper reflection on a number of initiatives that it was planning. In accordance with the conclusions of the Lisbon European Council the Commission will supplement this with a report to the December 1993 European Council on the results of its review of certain Community rules with a view to adapting them to the subsidiarity principle.

1. The Commission's first priority was to review all proposals pending before the Council and Parliament in the light of the subsidiarity principle. It reviewed each principle in terms both of the need-for-action criterion and of the intensity criterion — that is to say, proportionality of resources deployed to objectives pursued.

    (a)   The Commission has come to the conclusion that certain of its proposals were not fully warranted in terms either of value added by Community action or of comparative efficiency in relation to other possibilities of action in national or international contexts.

In this spirit it recently withdrew three proposals for Directives:—

— compulsory indication of nutritional values on the packaging of foodstuffs;
— radio frequencies for land-based telecommunications with aircraft; and
— radio frequencies for remote-processing facilities in road transport.

After the proper contacts, notably with Parliament, it is further considering withdrawing the following proposals:—

— measures proposed at the time of the Gulf crisis in the event of oil supply and stock difficulties in the Community;
— conditions in which animals are kept in zoos (there will be a proposal for a Recommendation on this subject at a later date);
— radio frequencies for the co-ordinated introduction of digital short-range radio communications;
— indirect taxation transactions in securities;
— amendments to the Sixth VAT Directive;
— higher tax-free allowances for fuel in the tanks of utility vehicles;
— VAT on ships' supplies;
— temporary importation of motor vehicles;
— classification of documents of Community institutions;
— network of information centres on agricultural markets and quality standards.

(b) The Commission has concluded, notably following debates in Parliament and the Council, that certain pending proposals tend to go into excessive detail in relation to the objective pursued.

It is accordingly planning to revise a number of them so that they establish general principles to be given more direct form by the Member States:—

— public takeover bids;
— common definition of the concept of Community shipowner;
— comparative advertising;
— labelling of shoes;
— liability of suppliers services;
— protection of natural persons in relation to data processed via digital telecommunications networks.

2. The Commission has also identified several families of existing rules and regulations which it intends to scrutinize as part of its programme for 1993.

As far as technical standards are concerned, a series of directives embodying excessively detailed specifications could be streamlined and replaced, under the new approach to harmonization, by minimum requirements to be met by products circulating freely within the Community. The directives in question relate in the main to foodstuffs (preserves, natural mineral waters, honey, coffee extracts, fruit juices). The Commission will also propose that the scope of certain directives be clarified. Although adopted under the new approach to harmonization, these texts (the low tension and machinery directives for instance) present problems of overlapping.

In the area of qualifications, the Commission will review the already quite old directives on certain regulated occupations to facilitate implementation and reinforce mutual recognition.

On the environment, the Commission intends to simplify, consolidate and update existing texts, particularly those on air and water, to take new knowledge and technical progress into account.

On agriculture, with particular reference to the clearance of accounts, the Commission intends to give national authorities more responsibility for applying Community legislation by allowing them, under certain conditions, to negotiate settlements with individuals.

As to animal welfare, acession by all the Member States to the European Convention on the Protection of Animals Kept for Farming Purposes means that there is no point in retaining Council directives introducing very strict standards, at Parliament's request, for the protection of pigs, calves and laying hens. However, minimum Community rules on animal welfare will be needed to guarantee fair competition and freedom of movement.

Turning to social policy, the Commission considers that the group of directives based on Article 118a of the Treaty is too recent to warrant re-examination. Instead its priority will be to supplement them by implementing all the provisions of the Charter of the Fundamental Social Rights of Workers. However, early steps will have to be taken to simplify and codify the body of older regulations on the free movement of workers.

3. Finally the Commission can say that, following consultations with interested parties, it intends to abandon certain initiatives that had been planned.

It will not, for instance, be going ahead with proposals on the harmonization of vehicle number plates or the regulation of gambling. Similarly, the Commission sees no need to continue preparatory work on the harmonization of certain technical standards (for instance, on dietary foods, second-hand machinery, structures and equipment for funfairs and theme parks, mechanical fixing and bolts in particular).

In more general terms the Commission is intending to use its monopoly of the right of initiative by declining to accept requests made by the Council at informal meetings that it make proposals for Directives. In the same spirit it will be tougher about rejecting amendments proposed by the Council and Parliament that run counter to the proportionality rule or would unnecessarily complicate Directives or Recommendations that are in fact justified under the need-for-action criterion.

Part Three: Transparency — Implementation of the Birmingham Declaration

Access to the Work of the Council

The process of opening up the work of the Council will start in the following areas:—

(a) Open Debates on Work Programme and on Major Initiatives of Community Interest
(i) Open orientation debates on relevant Presidency or Commission work programmes, in both the General Affairs Council and the ECOFIN Council. The timing will be for decision by the Presidency.

(ii) There should be regular open debates on major issues of Community interest. It will be for the Presidency, any Member State or the Commission to propose issues for open debate. The decision will be taken by the Council on a case by case basis.

(b) Legislation
Major new legislative proposals will, whenever appropriate, be the subject of a preliminary open debate, in the relevant Council, on the basis of the Commission's legislative proposal. It will be for the Presidency, any Member State or the Commission to propose specific subjects for a debate. The decision will be taken by the Council on a case by case basis. Negotiations on legislation in the framework of the Council shall remain confidential.

(c) Publication of Voting Records
When a formal vote is taken in Council, the record of the vote (including explanations of vote where delegations request these) shall be published.

(d) The decision on holding an open debate on a specific item under point (a)(ii) and (b) shall be taken by unanimity.

(e) 'Public access' will be achieved by televising the debate for viewing in the press area of the Council building.

Information on the Role of the Council

(a) Transparency on the Council's decisions

— Extension to all Council formations of the practice, established over the years in most Councils, of publishing a full description in the Press release of the conclusions reached by the Council (exceptions being made for cases where such information would damage the interests of the Member States, the Council, or the Community — eg. negotiating mandates). More systematic emphasis on publication of explanatory summaries concerning important "A" points adopted at the Council. Greater efforts to be made when drafting conclusions to make them understandable to the public.

— Better background information on Council decisions (eg. objective, history, link to other subjects) to be made available, if possible for distribution at pre-Council press briefings, in the form of background notes prepared by the Secretariat in user-friendly terms. This initiative could be extended in the future to cover matters relating to Common Foreign and Security policy and Internal and Justice Affairs, taking into account the specific need for confidentiality in some areas.

— Systematic background pre-Council press briefings by Presidency, assisted by Council Secretariat (today not all Presidencies hold such briefings and often they are limited to the national Press corps).

— Publication of the common positions established by the Council under the procedures of Articles 189b and 189c and the explanatory memorandum accompanying them.

— It is important to make all information material available rapidly in all Community languages.

(b) Increase in general information on the role and the activities of the Council

— The annual report, which is currently published after long delays, to be published from now on early in the new year on the responsibility of the Secretary General. Aim to make it more interesting and more understandable to the public — and complementary to, rather than duplicating, the Commission's annual report. There should also be a short summary aimed at broad circulation.

— Increase in the Council's information activities in general including a reinforcement of the Press Service. Stepping up of the already quite intensive information activity (group visits) performed by the services of the Secretariat. Establishing a programme for visits of journalists — particularly EC news editors — not based in Brussels (in co-operation with Commission).

(c)   Cooperation and more Rapid Transmission of Material

—   Activating the existing information group of the Council and extending it to the other institutions with a view to developing coordinated information strategies;

—   Cooperation between Member States and the Community institutions in the information field.
—   Use of new communication technologies: data bases, electronic-mail for making information available outside Council meeting places (Brussels/ Luxembourg).

Simplification of and Easier Access to Community Legislation

(a)   Making new Community legislation clearer and simpler
While the technical nature of most texts and the need to compromise among the various national positions often complicate the drafting process, practical steps should nevertheless be taken to improve the quality of Community legislation, such as the following:—

> (a) guidelines for the drafting of Community legislation should be agreed upon, containing criteria against which the quality of drafting of legislation would have to be checked;

> (b) delegations of member States should endeavour, at all levels of the Council proceedings, to check more thoroughly the quality of legislation;

> (c) the Council Legal Service should be requested to review draft legislative acts on a regular basis before they are adopted by the Council and make suggestions where necessary for appropriate redrafting in order to make such acts as simple and clear as possible;

> (d) the jurist-linguist group, which does the final legal editing of all legislation before it is adopted by the Council (with the participation of national legal experts), should give suggestions for simplifying and clarifying the language of the texts without changing their substance.

(b)   Making existing Community legislation more accessible
Community legislation can be made more readily accessible in a concise and intelligible form through a speedier and more organised use of consolidation and codification; an improvement of the CELEX database system should also be considered.

The two possible approaches—unofficial consolidation and official codification — must be pursued in parallel.[5]

(a)   The Office for Official Publications of the European Communities has an important role to play in respect of *unofficial consolidation*. Planning of this began some time ago and a new system will be operated as from 1993 on, whereby the consolidated version of all Community legislation undergoing amendments can be made automatically available following any such amendment; two years later, the system should be able to cover the whole of Community legislation (including past legislation) provided that there is adequate funding. Consolidated legislation should be immediately published (in the C-series of the *Official Journal*), possibly after adding the "considérants", and/or made available through CELEX.

(b)   *Official codification* is important because it provides legal security as to the law which is applicable at a certain moment concerning a specific issue. Since official codification can only be done through the relevant legislative procedures, priorities need to be established and an accelerated working method agreed upon between the three institutions which have legislative powers.

(i) Official codification should take place on the basis of agreed priorities. The Commission will propose such priorities in its work programme after appropriate consultation;

(ii) A jointly acceptable accelerated working method should be sought allowing codified Community law, (replacing existing legislation without changing its substance) to be adopted in a speedy and efficient way; a consultative group composed of the legal services of the Commission, the Council and the Parliament would help to carry out the necessary ground work to permit the adoption of codified Community legislation as rapidly as possible under the Community's normal decision-making procedure.

The CELEX data system should be improved with a view to:— [6]

(a) catching up with the delay as to existing legislation, and feeding the database in the Greek, Spanish and Portugese languages;

(b) making the system a more user friendly and accessible to the public. The necessary financial means should be available.

---

(1)   See Articles A and B of the Treaty on European Union.

(2)   Articles 118a, 126, 127, 128, 129, 129a, 129b, 130 and 130g of the EC Treaty, Article 2 of the Agreement on social policy. Furthermore, Article K.3(2)b directly incorporates the principle of subsidiarity.

(3)   The new Articles 126 to 129 of the EC Treaty in the area of education, vocational training and youth, culture and public health will explicitly rule out harmonisation of laws and regulations of Member States. It follows that the use of Article 235 for harmonisation measures

in pursuit of the specific objectives laid down in Article 126 to 129 will be ruled out. This does not mean that the pursuit of other Community objectives through Treaty articles other than 126 to 129 might not produce effects in these areas. Where Articles 126, 128 and 129 refer to "incentive measures", the Council considers that this expression refers to Community measures designed to encourage cooperation between Member States or to support or supplement their action in the areas concerned, including where appropriate through financial support for Community programmes or national or cooperative measures designed to achieve the objectives of these articles.

(4)   In the course of this examination, any Member State has the right to require that the examination of a proposal which raises Article 3b issues be inscribed on the provisional agenda of a Council in accordance with Article 2 of the Council's rules of procedure. If such examination, which will include all relevant points of substance covered by the Commission proposal, shows that the majority required for the adoption of the act does not exist, the possible outcomes include amendments of the proposal by the Commission, continued examination by the Council with a view to putting it into conformity with Article 3b or a provisional suspension of discussion of the proposal. This does not prejudice Member States or Commission rights under Article 2 of the Council's rules of procedure nor the Council obligation to consider the opinion of the European Parliament.

(5)   A clear distinction must be made between:—

— unofficial consolidation which consists in editorial assembling, outside any legislative procedure, of the scattered parts of legislation on a specific issue, which has no legal effect and which leaves all such parts in force (see for instance the consolidated text of the Financial Regulation, OJ C80 of 25/03/91 p.1); and official codification which is achieved through the adoption of a formal legislative Community act through the relevant procedures, while repealing all pre-existing texts (see, for instance, the Council Regulation on the common organisation on the market in fishery products, OJ L354 of 23/12/91 p.1).

(6)   The CELEX system (automated documentation on Community law) was set up in 1970 as an interinstitutional computerised documentation system and was made available to the public in 1981; it contains the entire body of EC law. On 13 November 1991, the Council adopted a resolution on the re-organisation of the operating structures of CELEX with a view to enhancing its effectiveness (OJ C308 of 28/11/91 p.2).

European Charter of Local Self-Government

Established by the Council of Europe at Strasbourg on 15 October 1985

PREAMBLE

The member States of the Council of Europe, signatory hereto,

Considering that the aim of the Council of Europe is to achieve a greater unity between its members for the purpose of safeguarding and realising the ideals and principles which are their common heritage;

Considering that one of the methods by which this aim is to be achieved is through agreements in the administrative field;

Considering that the local authorities are one of the main foundations of any democratic regime;

Considering that the right of citizens to participate in the conduct of public affairs is one of the democratic principles that are shared by all members States of the Council of Europe;

Convinced that it is at the local level that this right can be most directly exercised;

Convinced that the existence of local authorities with real responsibilities can provide an administration which is both effective and close to the citizen;

Aware that the safeguarding and reinforcement of local self-government in the different European countries is an important contribution to the construction of a Europe based on the principles of democracy and the decentralisation of power;

Asserting that this entails the existence of local authorities endowed with democratically constituted decision-making bodies and possessing a wide degree of autonomy with regard to their responsibilities, the ways and means by which those responsibilities are exercised and the resources required for their fulfilment,

Have agreed as follows:—

Article 1

The Parties undertake to consider themselves bound by the following articles in the manner and to the extent prescribed in Article 12 of this Charter.

PART I

Article 2
Constitutional and legal foundation
for legal self-government

The principle of local self-government shall be recognised in domestic legislation, and where practicable in the constitution.

Article 3
Concept of local self-government

1. Local self-government denotes the right and the ability of local authorities, within the limits of the law, to regulate and manage a substantial share of public affairs under their own responsibility and in the interests of the local population.

2. This right shall be exercised by the councils or assemblies composed of members freely elected by secret ballot on the basis of direct, equal, universal suffrage, and which may possess executive organs responsible to them. This provision shall in no way affect recourse to assemblies of citizens, referendums or any other form of direct citizen participation where it is permitted by statute.

Article 4
Scope of local self-government

1. The basic powers and responsibilities of local authorities shall be prescribed by the constitution or by statute. However, this provision shall not prevent the attribution to local authorities of powers and responsibilities for specific purposes in accordance with the law.

2. Local authorities shall, within the limits of the law, have full discretion to exercise their initiative with regard to any matter which is not excluded from their competence nor assigned to any other authority.

3. Public responsibilities shall generally be exercised, in preference, by those authorities which are closest to the citizen. Allocation of responsibility to another authority should weigh up the extent and nature of the task and requirements of efficiency and economy.

4. Powers given to local authorities shall normally be full and exclusive. They may not be undermined or limited by another, central or regional, authority except as provided for by the law.

5. Where powers are delegated to them by a central or regional authority, local authorities shall, insofar as possible, be allowed discretion in adapting their exercise to local conditions.

6. Local authorities shall be consulted, insofar as possible, in due time and in an appropriate way in the planning and decision-making process for all matters which concern them directly.

Article 5
Protection of local authority boundaries

Changes in local authority boundaries shall not be made without prior consultation of the local communities concerned, possibly by means of a referendum where this is permitted by statute.

Article 6
Appropriate administrative structures
and resources for the tasks of local authorities

1. Without predjudice to more general statutory provisions, local authorities shall be able to determine their own internal administrative structures in order to adapt them to local needs and ensure effective management.
2. The conditions of service of local government employees shall be such as to permit the recruitment of high-quality staff on the basis of merit and competence; to this end adequate training opportunities, remuneration and career prospects shall be provided.

Article 7
Conditions under which responsibilities
at local level are exercised

1. The conditions of office of elected representatives shall provide for free exercise of their functions.
2. They shall allow for appropriate financial compensation for expenses incurred in the exercise of the office in question as well as, where appropriate, compensation for loss of earnings or remuneration for work done and corresponding social welfare protection.
3. Any functions and activities which are deemed incompatible with the holding of local elective office shall be determined by statute or fundamental legal principles.

Article 8
Administrative supervision of
local authorities' activities

1. Any administrative supervision of local authorities may only be exercised according to such procedures and in such cases as are provided for by the constitution or by statute.
2. Any administrative supervision of the activities of the local authorities shall normally aim only at ensuring compliance with the law and with constitutional principles. Administrative supervision may however be exercised with regard to expediency by higher-level authorities in respect of tasks the execution of which is delegated to local authorities.
3. Administrative supervision of local authorities shall be exercised in such a way as to ensure that the intervention of the controlling authority is kept in proportion to the importance of the interests which it is intended to protect.

Article 9
Financial resources of local authorities

1. Local authorities shall be entitled, within national economic policy, to adequate financial resources of their own, of which they may dispose freely within the framework of their powers.

2. Local authorities' financial resources shall be commensurate with the responsibilities provided for by constitution and the law.

3. Part at least of the financial resources of local authorities shall derive from local taxes and charges of which, within the limits of statute, they have the power to determine the rate.

4. The financial systems on which resources of local authorities are based shall be of a sufficiently diversified and buoyant nature to enable them to keep pace as far as practically possible with the real evolution of the cost of carrying out their tasks.

5. The protection of financially weaker local authorities calls for the institution of financial equalisation procedures or equivalent measures which are designed to correct the effects of the unequal distribution of potential sources of finance and of the financial burden they must support. Such procedures or measures shall not diminish the discretion local authorities may exercise their own sphere of responsibility.

6. Local authorities shall be consulted, in an appropriate manner, on the way in which redistributed resources are to be allocated to them.

7. As far as possible, grants to local authorities shall not be earmarked for the financing of specific projects. The provision of grants shall not remove the basic freedom of local authorities to exercise policy discretion within their own jurisdiction.

8. For the purpose of borrowing for capital investment, local authorities shall have access to the national capital market within the limits of the law.

Article 10
Local authorities' right to associate

1. Local authorities shall be entitled, in exercising their powers, to cooperate and, within the framework of the law, to form consortia with other local authorities in order to carry out tasks of common interest.

2. The entitlement of local authorities to belong to an association for the protection and promotion of their common interests and to belong to an international association of local authorities shall be recognised in each state.

3. Local authorities shall be entitled, under such conditions as may be provided for by the law, to cooperate with their counterparts in other states.

Article 11
Legal protection of local self-government

Local authorities shall have the right of recourse to a judicial remedy in order to secure free exercise of their powers and respect for such principles of local self-government as are enshrined in the constitution or domestic legislation.